Days of the Lord

Days of the Lord

III. *Summer and Fall*

Edited by

William G. Storey

HERDER AND HERDER

1966
HERDER AND HERDER NEW YORK
232 Madison Avenue, New York 10016

Original French edition: *Les Jours du Seigneur,* edited by
P. Drujon and R. Cappanera, Editions du Témoignage
Chrétien, Paris; German edition: *Die Tage des Herrn,*
edited by Heinrich Bacht, S.J., Josef Knecht, Frankfurt
am Main.

The other volumes of *Days of the Lord* are:
I. Winter
II. Spring

Grateful acknowledgment is hereby expressed to those
publishers who have granted permission to reprint selec-
tions from their works. A detailed list of these works appears in the Reference Table at the end of this book.

Nihil obstat: William J. Collins, S.T.L.
                Censor Librorum
Imprimatur: ✠ Ernest J. Primeau
                Bishop of Manchester
                April 14, 1966

The Nihil obstat and Imprimatur are official declarations
that a book or pamphlet is considered to be free of doc-
trinal or moral error. No implication is contained therein
that those who have granted the Nihil obstat and Imprimatur agree with the contents, opinions, or statements
expressed.

Library of Congress Catalog Card Number: 65–21941
© 1966 by Herder and Herder, Incorporated
Manufactured in the United States of America

Contents

TEMPORAL

SANCTORAL

Temporal

AUTUMN DAY

Lord, it is time. The summer was too long.
Lay now thy shadow over the sundials,
and on the meadows let the winds blow strong.

Bid the last fruit to ripen on the vine;
allow them still two friendly southern days
to bring them to perfection and to force
the final sweetness in the heavy wine.

Who has no house now will not build him one.
Who is alone now will be long alone,
will waken, read, and write long letters
and through the barren pathways up and down
restlessly wander when dead leaves are blown.

                              RAINER MARIA RILKE [1]

The Weekly Easter after Pentecost

> In Jesus all times find their consummation.
> Just as he gave us his birth so we share his resurrection.
>
> PAUL CLAUDEL [1]

Pentecost is the finale of the mysteries of salvation; henceforth we await only the Parousia, the Lord's return, which will forever consummate our participation in his glory. But despite its unexpectedness, at once tragic and triumphal, this return will not mark as radical a transformation in our souls as that wrought by baptism. It will only ratify and make manifest in the full light of the day of judgment [1 Cor. 3, 13–15] a work accomplished day after day in the secret recesses of the heart and, moreover, in the whole Church, namely, the personal and collective transformation in Christ of all the members of his body.

CHRIST THE VICTOR AND THE HOLY SPIRIT

The Holy Spirit is, as it were, the swelling leaven of this progressive growth in Christ and the seal or brand which marks us out as God's own and guarantees the final accomplishment of this transformation in Christ. [2 Cor. 1, 22; 5, 5; Eph. 1, 13–14; see Rom. 8, 23] We do not await a future reign of the Holy Spirit, as certain sects[2] have imagined from time to time; the age of the

[1] Paul Claudel, "Hymne de la Pentecôte," in *Corona Benignitatis Anni Dei,* Paris, Gallimard, 1920, p. 37.

[2] Montanists in the second century; "Spirituals" of various sorts,

11

Spirit was inaugurated on the birthday of the Church, and the Acts of the Apostles, as it is often put, are the Gospel of the Holy Spirit. With the glorious mysteries we have entered upon the "last days," and now that the decisive interventions of God in history have been accomplished, the whole of Christian life is eschatological; henceforth a thousand years are as but a single day. [1 Cor. 10, 11; Heb. 1, 2; 2 Pet. 3, 8]

Because we have adopted the terminology of certain Frankish liturgists of the eighth century[3] and speak of "the Sundays after Pentecost" does not mean that we have left this mystery behind us in the way one passes by a landmark in history like the Hegira of Mohammed or the Coronation of Charlemagne. One can speak of the Moslem era or the Carolingian era or even of the Christian era, but in this latter case Christians do not consider the God-Man to belong to a bygone past. Despite the apparent monotony of this long series of "Green Sundays," each Sunday after Pentecost commemorates and celebrates unceasingly Christ's victory over sin and death and hell; and the witness and agent who brings this victory to its full term in us is the Spirit whom Jesus has sent us from his home in gloryland. [Lk. 24, 49; Jn. 15, 26; 16, 7–8. 14; Acts 1, 4–5; Eph. 4, 10–12; Rom. 8, 16] Each of these Sundays is, then, in the deepest sense, the Lord's Day.[4]

THE MYSTERY OF SUNDAY

Despite the special emphasis borne by so many Sundays of the Church's year (for example, those of Advent), each Sunday should properly maintain its original character of being the weekly feast commemorating and liturgically re-enacting the pas-

---

many of them disciples of Joachim of Flora, in the thirteenth century; Adventists and Pentecostals in the nineteenth century.

[3] The oldest surviving witness to this usage is the Sacramentary of Gellone (around 780 A.D.).

[4] The connection between the resurrection and the mystery of the Holy Spirit is very closely made in the old liturgy. Originally, Pentecost Sunday itself brought paschaltide to a close, thus completing without further extension the greater octave of Easter, the week of weeks (fifty days).

chal mystery. During the time after Pentecost the Sunday exists, in a sense, in its pure state as this weekly celebration of the resurrection of Christ by God's own people [1 Pet. 2, 9].[5]

The Sabbath of the Old Testament modeled man's weekly day of rest upon that rest which God is depicted as taking at the conclusion of the six days of creation. By inviting man to lay aside his laborious tasks, which are so necessary and yet so transitory, in favor of divine contemplation, the Sabbath rest devoted to God reminded him of the primacy of end over means, of what the ancients called the delightful over the merely useful; [6] thus he would not become absorbed in the things of time to the possible exclusion of the things of eternity. The Sabbath reminded man that his ultimate destiny is immanent in the very becoming which characterizes his existence as a creature of time. To live for a whole day each week with the thought of God is to anticipate eternal life by enjoying a communion with the divine repose, a repose which is not a do-nothing absence of work, but a sharing in that living peace of wisdom and freedom characteristic of the eternal mansions.

The Old Testament, however, had access to this spiritual climate only obscurely and figuratively, that is, in prophetic fashion simply. To the wholly temporary rest of the seventh day there succeeded the first day of a work-week during which man was commanded to pursue the still uncompleted work of creation. But the resurrection of Christ, on the day after the Sabbath, became the "eighth day"; [7] while Israel, with still veiled eyes, resumed

[5] The Byzantine liturgy still maintains the ancient Christian custom (observed by Aetheria at Jerusalem in the fourth century) of reading a Gospel of the resurrection during the course of the night office. It is quite possible that the Gospel which St. Benedict legislated for at the conclusion of vigils each Sunday was also that of the resurrection. St. Caesarius of Arles in his rule of the same sixth century had a similar custom.

[6] Cicero was the first to employ the terms *"uti"* and *"frui"* or *"utile"* and *"honestum"* in these precise senses (*De finibus* II, 14; *De officus* III, 7; *Pro Roscio Amerino* 45, 13). Thanks to St. Ambrose and St. Augustine, this distinction became a major theme of Christian reflection and prevented men from making work an end in itself as many modern philosophers, especially the Marxists, are tempted to do.

[7] In the early part of the second century the so-called Epistle of

13

work again on the first day of the week, Jesus passed from the repose of death, which was his last Sabbath observance, to the living repose of his glory. And this "passage" or passing over without return, the true passover, brings to completion finally and forever, world without end, the "week" of his labor and his passion.

Each member of Christ in his turn will share in this victorious bridging of time and eternity, breaking with the old Sabbath observance in favor of the new day. Christians certainly could not rest content with the Sabbath and its meaning any more than they could with all the rest of the former and provisory economy of salvation of which it was so signal a part. [Gal. 4, 9–10; Col. 2, 16–17] The *Dies dominica*[8] excels the Sabbath and creates the Christian week. The Lord's Day was the original feast day and was for a long time perhaps its only feast.[9] Thus the Christian, reborn from above by means of the paschal mystery made operative in him through his Easter baptism and communion, is from that moment on summoned to a great and life-long pilgrimage. He travels from the resurrection of Christ, which is ever present for him in the liturgical celebration of each Sunday, towards his own resurrection, which the Risen Lord sketches out in him step by step. In the Sunday Eucharist, which he offers and receives as food for his journey, the Christian discovers both the life-giving means and the promise of everlasting life. [Jn. 6, 54–56] Any Christian who no longer expects and strives for this resurrection calls into question that of Christ himself. [1 Cor. 15, 13–20]

Barnabas (8–9) inaugurated this expression and gave it currency: "Your present Sabbaths are not acceptable to me, but that [Sabbath] is which I have made, when giving rest to all things, I shall make a new beginning on the eighth day, that is, a beginning of a new world. That is why we celebrate so joyfully the eighth day, the day on which Jesus rose from the dead, manifested himself, and ascended into heaven."

[8] The *Dies dominica* or Lord's Day was distinguished in New Testament times from the *Dies Domini* or Day of the Lord, meaning the day of his return, the day of the Parousia.

[9] See *The Constitution on the Sacred Liturgy,* Chapter V, Article 106.

For all this emphasis on "the theology of glory," as it has been called, we must not be led to suspect that "the theology of the way and of the cross" is thereby emptied of all meaning. Embracing the sense of a mystery is never a simplistic evasion, as certain Christians of Thessalonica, for example, imagined. [2 Thes. 2, 1–2; 3, 6–12] During the first centuries of Christianity Sunday inherited little or nothing, sociologically speaking, from the Sabbath, as it was to do later on under the Christian empire; and the eighth day was at one and the same time the first day of the week. Although the Judaeo-Christians still clung to the Sabbath rest, other Christians began each work-week on the Lord's Day,[10] which was at once the commemoration of his resurrection and a continual expectation of his Parousia. The entire inner meaning of the Lord's Day and of the Christian week resides in this symbiosis of time and eternity, of life *in via* and life *in patria,* of the time of struggle and the time of victory and perpetual peace. The life of the mystical body of Christ is a continuous celebration of the Easter mystery, a "passing over" which endures from the day of our baptismal regeneration to the end of our lives; or better, which coincides with all human history since Jesus came forth from the tomb.

Such is the Christian paradox as St. Paul and the Book of Revelation present it. The world does not seem changed. Under the pressure of sin death still breaks in with rhythmic regularity upon the tumultuous events of history in the same way the seasons interrupt the orderly flow of events. The liturgy understands all this very well, bewailing and sharing our griefs as well as making room for the joy of the harvest festivals. And yet in the midst of the very ordinary events of human existence, new men lead a new life. Their incorporation in Christ makes them members of the Risen One in such indisputable fashion that they are humbly aware that by faith his victory is theirs too. *Behold the victory*

[10] Although earlier attempts had been made, the first measures in favor of the Sunday rest stem from Constantine. Despite imperial, royal, and ecclesiastical legislation, however, the Sunday repose was interpreted much less rigidly than under the Old Law, and it was not until Carolingian times in Europe that Sabbatarianism, properly speaking, entered the lives of Christians.

which overcomes the world, our faith. [1 Jn. 5, 4] The master had promised that it would be so [Jn. 16, 22 and 33]; the beloved disciple bears witness that in truth it is.

Discouragement, hardness of heart, anxiety and despair, all those things which make men forget their native grandeur and vocation, are now left behind. The "new race" [11] which has appeared, their radiant faces reflecting like a mirror the glory of the Lord, are even now in the process of transfiguration. [2 Cor. 3, 18] Following in his footsteps and through his gracious help, they become capable of transforming a very ordinary life into a divine life, the trials and tribulations of everyday into a joyous offering, death into victory.[12] Like so many of the early martyrs, Bishop Cyprian of Carthage sketched for us in words of fire the picture of an Easter man, when he proclaimed to a persecutor: "Strong hope and firm faith flourish among us; standing erect in the midst of a world falling into ruins, with unshaken courage and joyful patience, our souls are always sure of God." [13]

Have the aims and aspirations of our day-to-day life ever found better expression? And yet a veritable crowd of martyrs and saints has borne the same witness to the Risen Lord. Although the feasts of such witnesses were not ranked with the principal solemnities of the liturgical cycle,[14] they came to be admitted rather easily into the calendar of the summer months. Are they not incomparable witnesses to the victory of Christ? In the modern liturgical calendar, after the Church lovingly considers the hidden treasures of her spouse (feasts of the Trinity, Corpus

[11] *Epistle to Diognetus.*

[12] "When killed we conquer." Tertullian, *Apology* 50, 3. The early Acts of the Martyrs are replete with these and similar formulas. They can all be summed up in the Latin Christian proverb: *"Vincit qui patitur":* "He who suffers comes out a conqueror."

[13] *Ad Demetrianum* 20, written probably in 252, seven years after his conversion and three years after his consecration as a bishop. The passage has a strong Stoic ring to it, but one illuminated by Christian joy.

[14] Even in the late eighth century the lectionary of Alcuin, which remained faithful to the Roman tradition, contained only two martyr saints between February 1 and May 1, St. Agatha (February 5) and St. Valentine.

16

Christi, the Sacred Heart) [15] towards the end of June the Church hears again that *launch out into the deep* [16] which will conduct her from apostle to martyr, from virgin to confessor to the glory of All Saints, a fitting conclusion to her liturgical year, and to the feasts of the Dedication of Churches (November 9 and 18) [17] which prophesy her final splendor, a splendor already anticipated in the feast of the assumption of Mary who is her mother and her image. Thanks to the liturgical reforms of the twentieth century, the saints will no longer find themselves in the "humiliating" position of having their feasts replace the Lord's Day! Nevertheless, the old Roman calendar [18] of centuries gone by liked to tie in the Sundays after Pentecost with certain great feasts as liturgical landmarks: those of Peter and Paul, Lawrence, Cyprian, or the Archangel Michael, thus willingly celebrating the victory of Christ in conjunction with those of the saints, his true trophies.

[15] Although these superb mysteries had been expressed and lived out liturgically from the earliest times, they had not had special feasts as such. There had been a votive Mass of the Holy Trinity in existence since the ninth century, but general acceptance was difficult until it was imposed as a feast by the Pope in 1334. The Preface of the Trinity, although of earlier origin, only became common in the seventeenth century and was not formally sanctioned until 1759 by Clement XIII. This "Trinitarianization" of the Green Sundays has unfortunately resulted in a de-emphasis of their paschal character; modern liturgists are asking for the restoration of the Common Preface with paschal motifs. Corpus Christi appeared in the thirteenth century as part of the "communion of the eye" replacement of actual holy communion which was on the wane. The feast of the Sacred Heart was a seventeenth-century reply to the cold austerities of Jansenist naturalism.

[16] Gospel of the fourth Sunday after Pentecost, called in the oldest Roman lectionary "Sunday before the Feast of the Apostles [Peter and Paul]."

[17] Dedication anniversaries of the Roman basilicas of the Savior (St. John Lateran) and of Peter and Paul (Vatican). Note especially the epistle and the Breviary hymns of these feasts.

[18] The Würzburg lectionary (seventh century) has seven Sundays after Peter and Paul, five after Lawrence, six others after Cyprian. The Paduan Gregorian Sacramentary has a similar structure except that it prefers the feast of St. Michael (September 29) to that of St. Cyprian.

17

For the Church militant it is joy, indeed, to pursue its course through history surrounded by *so great a cloud of witnesses.* [Heb. 12, 1]

The splendor of those who have preceded us to the heavenly city should not, however, cause us to forget that the entire Christian people must show forth in their lives that Christ has risen. Ernest Lavisse,[19] a rationalist of the old school, once avowed that while he was still uncertain as to what had taken place on Easter Sunday morning, "I do know, however, that on that day a race of men was born which will never see death. *Having risen from the dead Christ will die no more."* [Rom. 6, 9] Despite the insight betrayed by this assertion, Lavisse could hardly have suspected the full import of his words or fathomed the spiritual depths in which this resurrection takes place. Certainly, resurrection means a rising from a tomb, but it also means deliverance from that servitude which the fear of death brings [Heb. 2, 15], victory over the sting of death which is sin [1 Cor. 15, 56; Rom. 5, 12], and even the surmounting, lovingly and joyously, of the habitual menace of sinning. Born-again Christians can confidently assert that they are truly *dead to sin but alive to God in Christ Jesus.* [Rom. 6, 11] This is what St. Leo the Great thought and preached to his people:

> Although we are only saved by way of anticipation and still live in a mortal body subject to corruption, yet it is correct to say that we live no longer according to the flesh if carnal affections no longer have the mastery over us; it is fitting indeed to lay aside the name of that whose will we no longer obey [that is, the flesh]. . . . Let the people of God acknowledge that they are in Christ a new creature [2 Cor. 5, 17] and let them strive to understand by whom they have been received and whom he received. What has been made new should not return to the unstable and obsolete ways of the past.[20]

Or as St. Augustine put it: "Listen to the Apostle telling us: *If you have risen with Christ, seek the things that are above. . . .*

[19] Quoted in J. and J. Tharaud, *Notre cher Péguy,* 1926, p. 268.
[20] Sermon 71, 5–6; *PL* 54:389.

For you are dead. [Col. 3, 1. 3] He means that if we live as we should, we are both dead and risen." [21]

The spiritual masters of the French School of spirituality revived this grand patristic theme and popularized it in the seventeenth century. "Truly," as one of them taught, "the members of the body share in the dispositions of their Head, and it is impossible for them not to live of his life. Because we have the honor of being the members of Jesus Christ, and Jesus is risen and we with him, we must at present lead a heavenly life like his and behave ourselves here below as citizens of another world." [22] So preoccupied with spiritual purity, however, were such writers, that they may have overdone their emphasis on the eschatological aspect of Easter and have tried to transport Christians a little too soon to the purely spiritual realms.[23] Nevertheless, by infusing prayer, the apostolate, asceticism, and sacrifice with the spirit of Resurrection, they tried to make it possible for Christians to face up to all aspects of life, both bitter and sweet, with a Resurrection mentality, as members of Christ who died and rose again. They were only trying to repeat what St. Paul did for the neophytes of the first age of Christianity. [Eph. 2, 6; Col. 3, 1–3; Rom. 6, 4]

[21] Sermon 231, 3; *PL* 38:1105.

[22] Saint-Jure, *L'union avec Jésus-Christ dans ses principaux mystères,* VI, 3 (1st ed. of 1860, p. 254 J. J. Olier often dwelt upon this doctrine: "Christians who are brought to perfection in Jesus Christ lead a divine life; they are no longer themelves, they are other Christs living interiorly by his life and resurrection. . . . God has seized possession of them; he has, so to speak, changed them into himself. When he says: 'I will that. . . ,' his creatures absorbed in him say at the same moment: 'I will that. . . .' They never say: 'Because you will it, my God, I also will it,' but: 'I *do* as you will.' They carry out what God orders without going through a process of obedience, so to say, because their wills are completely swallowed up in God's" (*Pensées choisies,* ed. G. Letourneau, 2nd ed., 1922, pp. 52–53). In the twentieth century Abbot Columba Marmion, O.S.B., is the principal teacher of these essential truths in *Christ in His Mysteries* (10th ed., St. Louis, B. Herder, 1939).

[23] For example, in his *Catechism of the Interior Life,* Olier says: "The state of holiness into which a risen soul enters implies a separation from all creatures in the present world" (I Part, Lesson 24). If this were true as so baldly stated, Easter would become something

19

The "new life" in Christ proclaimed by Paul so vigorously was certainly no different than that of the original Good News. Although *heaven is our home* [Phil. 3, 20], this must not become a pretext for neglecting the example and words of Christ himself. The beatitudes he promulgated and lived here below and the "new" commandment of love shall not pass away and are an anticipation in this life of the world to come. Jesus himself, as a citizen of both worlds, let his favorite three disciples catch a glimpse of his glory on the Mount of Transfiguration, but for all that descended onto the plain again to take up his mission of living and proclaiming the Gospel.

Thus the fact that we are Easter men sharing in Jesus' paschal existence, cannot dispense us from ready and constant recourse to the words and acts of Jesus recorded in the Gospels. In this sense it is true to say with Tertullian that the coming of Christ has put an end to other searching: "We need no curiosity after Christ nor inquiry after the Gospel." [24] Even the Spirit who is to lead us into all truth limits his role to recalling to our minds the teachings of the Master. [Jn. 14, 26; 16, 12–15] In order to grasp fully their basic newness we must listen to the Gospel as sons of the resurrection. [Lk. 20, 36] We must attempt to put ourselves in the spiritual climate of the first Christians who heard the Good News from the lips of the "evangelists" in the course of their weekly assembly on the Lord's Day.

FEAST OF THE HOLY TRINITY

(CELEBRATED ON THE FIRST SUNDAY AFTER PENTECOST)

After Christmas, Easter, and Whitsuntide, comes Trinity Sunday, and the weeks that follow; and in like manner, after our soul's anxious travail; after the birth of the Spirit; after trial and temp-

---

purely of the next life. But Easter takes place *in* the world; it belongs to the earth, it smells of the earth, even if it is not of this world. See G. Aubourg, *Sang et Gloire,* Bruges, Desclée de Brouwer, 1942, p. 19.

[24] *"Nobis curiositate opus non est post Christum, nec inquisitione post Evangelium"* (*De praescriptione* VII, 12).

tation; after sorrow and pain; after daily dyings to the world; after daily risings unto holiness; at length comes that *rest which remaineth unto the people of God.* [Heb. 4, 9] After the fever of life; after wearinesses and sicknesses; fightings and despondings; languor and fretfulness; struggling and failing, struggling and succeeding; after all the changes and chances of this troubled unhealthy state, at length comes death, at length the White Throne of God, at length the Beatific Vision. After restlessness comes rest, peace, joy; our eternal portion, if we be worthy; the sight of the Blessed Three, the Holy One; the Three that bear witness in heaven; in light unapproachable; in glory without spot or blemish; in power without *variableness, or shadow of turning.* [Jas. 1, 17] The Father God, the Son God, and the Holy Ghost God; the Father Lord, the son Lord, and the Holy Ghost Lord; the Father uncreate, the Son uncreate, and the Holy Ghost uncreate; the Father incomprehensible, the Son incomprehensible, and the Holy Ghost incomprehensible. For there is one Person of the Father, another of the Son, and another of the Holy Ghost; and such as the Father is, such is the Son, and such is the Holy Ghost; and yet there are not three Gods, nor three Lords, nor three incomprehensibles, nor three uncreated; but one God, one Lord, one uncreated, and one incomprehensible.

JOHN HENRY NEWMAN [2]

In the name of the Father and of the Son and of the Holy Spirit.

On the one hand, God is called the "Father." Not only because he loves us, his creatures, paternally (love which would not necessarily penetrate to the innermost depths of his being), but because he fathered a Son equal to himself. Not only creative, but self-creative, he pours out his essence in a Second Person Intimate: Thou; thus forming the illimitable plenitude of his Being into a substantial Word who goes forth from him and returns to him.

Then again God is called "Son." Not because he made himself the Child of Man, taking form from man's life and heart (this would not necessarily penetrate to the core of divine Being), but Son because he is the living image of his Sire, "begotten, not

21

made." In the Son, the mystery of the divine Father is made manifest: Face that confronts God's own as in a mirror. He is the Spoken Word of an omnipotent Speaker, Word that returns to the creative Mouth in the bliss of infinite fulfillment. Two countenances then in one God. Two Persons, distinct in all reality and truth, separated by their sacred, inexorable dignity, yet one God.

Between them exists something unknown to man that makes possible their existence as two separate Beings yet with one life, one essence unhampered by the limitations of self which protect and isolate all other life. Between Creator and Creator everything is open; the closed doors of individuality are non-existent. The given condition, likewise unknown to man, that makes this possible is of course perfection of person. Nothing created is completely self-possessed, and this lack is evinced by the creature's incapacity for perfect union with another creature, which only complete self-surrender could bring about. With God it is different. The sacred Two-in-God of whom we are speaking are entirely open to each other—so much so that they share a single life. The one lives so completely in the other, that there is not a pulsebeat, not a breath, not a spark that is not mutual. This must be the reason why each is so perfectly self-contained.

All this means that God is "Spirit"—not Understanding, Logic, Will, but Holy Spirit, *Pneuma*. It is in him, the Third Person of the Trinity, that Father and Son are powerfully individual, yet one. In the Spirit the Father engenders the clear image of himself in which he is "well pleased." In the Spirit, Jesus receives divine truth and reflects it back to the Father. In the Spirit, the Father pours out his essence, the Word, confident that in Jesus it will be invulnerable. In the Spirit, the Son receives the essence of his being from the Father, is his Word and yet Lord of himself.

This mutual exchange and autonomy in the Spirit is itself a Countenance. The Third Person who makes it possible for the One to find and possess himself completely in the Other is the Holy Spirit, who flashes through Scripture in the strange symbols of the descending Dove, Wind that blows where it will, mighty Tempest from the skies, and Tongues of flame. [Jn. 1, 32; 3, 8; Acts 2, 2–3]

But all is a great mystery, and the symbols only make us feel it

22

the more. It cannot be "explained." All we can do is to grope, reverently, in the darkness of Christ's words and existence.

ROMANO GUARDINI [3]

Daily life is Trinitarian life; it reveals the Father, the Son, and the Holy Spirit.

Let us live intensely our life of faith, hope, and charity; let us live this life intelligently, reflecting on it with an eagerness to learn. Let us develop in ourselves, to the utmost power of our will, the consciousness that we belong to the Word and the divine Thought; let us develop confidence in the Father and zeal for Him, and docility, love, and fervor in the Spirit. Then we shall come to some understanding, not in words and concepts, but in growth and life-giving light, of the mystery of the Father, the Son, and the Holy Ghost. In the "little way" of spiritual childhood, in adherence to the Church, and in devotedness to our neighbor, many a treasure of theology will be found.

Christ Himself, we may well judge, taught the mystery of the Trinity by His actions even more than by His words. Trinitarian formulas are rare in the Gospel, and there is hardly one more explicit than the formula of baptism in St. Matthew. The other passages that teach this truth, numerous though they may be, are accounts Christ gives of His conduct or of the conduct He requires of others. Such conduct is the main theme of His message. In the presence of the Twelve He always acted in function of the Trinity, if we may put it that way, that is, in a way that presupposed and implied the Trinity. In His dealings with God He always took, quite naturally and recognizably, the attitude of a Son in the presence of His Father, the attitude of one who receives everything he has and is, the attitude of one who relies on another for absolutely everything.

By the influence of His example and the power of His grace, far more than by His words, He has gradually instilled into the souls of His followers a similar attitude, an attitude of reference to the Father, of confidence in the Father, and of a wholehearted, supernatural, mysterious love. Under the action of the Spirit, this attitude enabled the disciples to understand the sense of His words, although their lives were already manifesting it, and also brought Christ's revelation to the dogmatic formulation given by the Church.

The same is true for the Christian. Meditation on the formulas of Nicaea and Constantinople, on the theological syntheses of St. Gregory, St. Augustine, and St. Thomas, and all that tradition has said about God's interior life, undoubtedly ought to impart to us a vivid understanding of the dogma of the Trinity. But that understanding is also, and particularly, fostered by acting in the way the Church recommends, by taking the attitude of adopted sons, and by living the life of faith, hope, and charity which, in Christ, unites us to the Word and, through the Word, to Him who is our Father and to Him who is our Spirit.

EMILE MERSCH [4]

FIRST SUNDAY AFTER PENTECOST
(USED ON THE WEEKDAYS AFTER TRINITY SUNDAY)

Be merciful as your Father is merciful. (Gospel)

One day when I was in Crete I received the hospitality of Carpus, a man famous for the extreme purity of his spirit. He was a man of a deep religious and contemplative cast, who never celebrated the holy mysteries without being consoled during his preliminary prayers with a sweet vision. He told me how one day he had been plunged into black despair when he learned that an unbeliever had stolen into the church and converted a Christian to paganism, and this had happened during the holy feasts which followed the baptism of the Christian.

So Carpus prayed for the two sinners and invoked the help of God, desiring that God should convert the pagan by His mercy, and bring the apostate back to the fold. He decided to spend the rest of his life exhorting them, putting an end to their doubts, so that after they have been punished for their temerity and folly, they might be brought back to the knowledge of God. And when nothing of the kind happened, Carpus fell into a fierce temper of indignation.

One evening he went to sleep, still overwhelmed with bitterness. It was his custom to awake during the night and compose himself for prayer. When the time for prayer had come, he awoke from his restless sleep, utterly cast down. He gave himself to prayer, but from his lips there came only a complaint against God, that it was unworthy of Him that He allowed the unbelievers, those who crossed the pathways of the Lord, to remain alive on earth. He begged God to send the lightning, and pitilessly destroy the two sinners. And he had hardly spoken when he observed that the house, where he was praying, trembled violently and then split suddenly in two.

Then it seemed to him that a vast and dazzling flame had been let down from Heaven, to fall at his feet, and in the depths of the open skies Jesus appeared, surrounded by a multitude of angels in human form. Carpus lifted his eyes, saw the miracle and trembled. Then he lowered his eyes, and saw beneath his feet that the ground had opened, revealing a vast and shadowy abyss. The two sinners he had cursed stood on the very edge of the abyss, trembling fearfully, barely able to hold one another up, in danger of falling. Out of the abyss terrible serpents were climbing towards them, winding round their feet, coiling round them, pulling them down, now biting them, now caressing them with their tails, in every conceivable manner attempting to fling them into the abyss. And as though the serpents were not powerful enough, men came running up, and they too attempted with blows to hurl the miserable sinners into the abyss, until at last the sinners, partly out of weariness, partly out of utter weakness and dejection, were close to being overthrown. Carpus watched all this in pure tranquillity of heart, observing the miracle before his eyes while forgetting the miracle he had observed a moment ago in the heavens. And as the contest was prolonged, tranquillity gave place to rage: he asked why their ruin should not be accomplished more quickly, and himself went to assist those who were trying to hurl the sinners down. And because he failed, his anger only increased and he cursed them.

And then it occurred to him to ask of the heavens why they

were still allowed to exist on the edge of the abyss. In the heavens the miracle was being continued. Jesus was looking down from the depths of the sky, but Jesus was filled with compassion. He rose from His throne, descended toward the sinners and stretched out His hand to them. Angels came down from heaven, and they held up the sinners. And Jesus turned to Carpus, saying: "Now lift your hands and strike Me, for I am ready to die once again for the salvation of men, and it would be sweet to me if I could be crucified, though committing no crime. Which do you prefer —to be hurled into the abyss, or to live with God and the angels, who are so good and friendly to men?"

DENIS THE AREOPAGITE [5]

Love your enemies. Bless those that curse you. Do good to those that wish you harm. If a man strikes you on your right cheek, turn the other cheek also towards him. If anyone would take your cloak, let him have your coat as well. Give to anyone who asks, and if anyone should take something from you, do not ask to have it back. Do to other men all that you have them do to you. Be merciful. Do not judge others, and you will not be judged. Forgive, and you will be forgiven by God. Do not consider the speck of dust in your brother's eye, but the beam in your own.

All these commandments have to do with charity, my children, and there can be nothing difficult for you to understand about them when you have realized, once for all, that all men together are but one family with God, their Creator and their Keeper, as their Father—their Father indeed in the same way towards all, for He loves them all incomparably more than the tenderest father in the world can love his children. Loving them thus, without exception, He wishes to see reigning among these sons of His, among His faithful, that concord, that love and tenderness, and, if needs be, that lenience and yielding gentleness, which a loving father always hopes to see among his children. He would have you give in to one another, help one another without stint; each yielding where your rights are concerned and never insisting upon them; letting the brother who is wrong or unfair have his way, so as to correct him by your gentleness and keep peace in the family, only praying for him that he may see his mistake and mend it.

So, you see, all these recommendations I have given you have but one purpose—to keep peace and love among all the brothers in the family of mankind. Always observe all these precepts, and let this principle from which they all come be deeply engraved in your souls, that all men are in fact and in truth *brothers* in God, their common Father, and God wishes them to regard each other, and love each other, and treat each other in every way, like tenderly loving brothers.

And be compassionate with one another. See My compassion for you, how I suffer with all suffering and pity all sufferers, how I sigh with this man and weep with that. I have pity on their mourning, their sickness, their anxieties, their hunger, their weakness, their ignorance; I not only did good to souls and bodies alike while on earth, but there remains in My Sacred Heart deep pity and compassion for all the ills of body and soul. Compassion is part of the love in every mortal heart, part of every human love.

CHARLES DE FOUCAULD [6]

CORPUS CHRISTI

(THURSDAY AFTER TRINITY SUNDAY)

The sacrifice of praise. (Canon)

The Psalms are not the Christian's supreme song of praise. He has one more song of praise to add to those of the Psalter, and one which is infinitely superior to them. He has that song of praise which we call the Holy Eucharist. The Eucharist is the specifically Christian praise psalm. That is precisely what its name means. The word Eucharist does not mean thanksgiving, as is often asserted, but praise. Beginning with the invocation *Gratias agamus Domino Deo nostro:* Let us praise the Lord our God, in the style of the praise psalms of the Psalter, the celebrant makes a solemn declaration of God's supreme and final and perfect work for our salvation. He has revealed Himself in a new and dazzling light, through the mystery of the Incarnate Word. He has attached the salvation of the human race to the tree of the

Cross, so that whence death sprang up, thence life might rise, and he who conquered by the tree, might by the tree also be conquered. He has provided us with our Paschal victim, Christ the true Lamb who has taken away the sins of the world, and by rising has restored our life. It is not surprising that the proclamation of such wonderful deeds leads us to interrupt the narrative praise psalm with the brief description of what God is: Holy, Holy, Holy, whose Glory fills heaven and earth. Then the narrative praise continues, proclaiming how Christ Our Lord, the night before he died, took bread and said: *This is my body*. The Christian declaration of God's wonderful deeds is accompanied by its offering also, and psalm and offering together constitute the sacrifice of praise, the Eucharist of which the poor will eat and rejoice.

THOMAS WORDEN [7]

Take and eat. This is my body. (Epistle)

This offering to God of bread and wine, of the food that we must eat in order to live, is our offering to him of ourselves, of our life and of the whole world. "To take in our hands the whole world as if it were an apple!" said a Russian poet. It is our Eucharist. It is the movement that Adam failed to perform, and that in Christ had become *the* very life of man. A movement of adoration and praise in which all joy and suffering, all beauty and all frustration, all hunger and all satisfaction, are referred to their ultimate End and become finally *meaningful*. Yes, to be sure, it is a sacrifice; but sacrifice is the most natural act of man, the very essence of his life. Man is a sacrificial being, because he finds his life in love, and love is sacrificial: it puts the "value," the very meaning of life in the other and gives life to the other, and in this giving, in this sacrifice, finds the meaning and joy of life.

We offer the world and ourselves to God. But we do it *in Christ* and *in remembrance of him*. We do it in Christ because he has already offered all that is to be offered to God. He has performed once and for all this Eucharist and nothing has been left unoffered. In him was Life—and this Life of all of us, he gave to God. The Church is all those who have been accepted into the

28

eucharistic life of Christ. And we do it again in remembrance of him because, as we offer again and again our life and our world to God, we discover each time that there is nothing else to be offered but Christ himself—the Life of the world, the fullness of all that exists. It is his Eucharist, and his is the Eucharist. As the prayer of offering says—"it is he who offers and it is he who is offered." The liturgy has led us into the all-embracing Eucharist of Christ, and has revealed to us that the only Eucharist, the only offering of the world is Christ. We come again and again with our lives to offer; we bring and "sacrifice"—that is, give to God—what he has given us; and each time we come to the End of all sacrifices, of all offerings, of all eucharist, because each time it is revealed to us that Christ has *offered* all that exists, and that he and all that exists has been offered in his offering of himself. We are included in the Eucharist of Christ and Christ is our Eucharist. . . .

And now, in this eucharistic offering in Christ of all things to the One to whom they belong and in whom alone they really exist—now this movement of ascension has reached its *end*. We are at the paschal table of the Kingdom. What we have offered—our food, our life, ourselves, and the whole world—we offered in Christ and as Christ because he himself has assumed our life and is our life. And now all this is given back to us as the gift of new life and therefore—necessarily—as food.

ALEXANDER SCHMEMANN [8]

Eucharistic celebration in the second century.

For all the favors we enjoy we bless the Creator of all, through His Son Jesus Christ and through the Holy Spirit. On the day which is called Sunday we have a common assembly of all who live in the cities or in the outlying districts, and the memoirs of the Apostles or the writings of the Prophets are read, as long as there is time. Then, when the reader has finished, the president of the assembly verbally admonishes and invites all to imitate such examples of virtue. Then we all stand up together and offer up our prayers, and, as we said before, after we finish our prayers, bread and wine and water are presented. He who presides like-

29

wise offers up prayers and thanksgivings, to the best of his ability, and the people express their approval by saying "Amen." The Eucharistic elements are distributed and consumed by those present, and to those who are absent they are sent through the deacons. The wealthy, if they wish, contribute whatever they desire, and the collection is placed in the custody of the president. With it he helps the orphans and widows, those who are needy because of sickness or any other reason, and the captives and strangers in our midst; in short, he takes care of all those in need.

ST. JUSTIN MARTYR [9]

SECOND SUNDAY AFTER PENTECOST

We have passed from death to life because we love our brothers. (Epistle)

The love Christ means is a live current that comes from God, is transmitted from person to person, and returns to God. It runs a sacred cycle reaching from God to an individual, from the individual to his neighbor, and back through faith to God. He who breaks the circuit at any point breaks the flow of love. He who transmits purely, however small a part of that love, helps establish the circuit for the whole.

ROMANO GUARDINI [10]

Brethren, let us strive to worship God by our love for each other. All effort is vain which does not lead to this . . . for the disciples of Christ are recognized by their mutual love. This is their characteristic mark: *By this shall all men know that you are my disciples.* [Jn. 13, 35] It was because of love that the Word was made Flesh and dwelt amongst us; for the Son of God became Man, freely and gladly enduring those sufferings which brought us life, in order to remake his creature, that human nature which the devil had shattered and torn apart. . . . This is the true and irreproachable Wisdom of God, which has for its ends the good and the true: the good, a kindness towards our

30

fellow men; the true, a worship of God in accordance with faith. These are the marks of that charity which unites men among themselves, and binds them to God.

Brethren, I knew a man who, in his love, made it his chief work to rescue his intimate companions from their evil thoughts and actions. This he would attempt to do by various means, as occasion offered; he would seek to influence one by his words, another by his acts of kindness. . . . I have known such a man weep over one, mourn for another—clearly, because he had taken upon himself their personality, and now charged himself with the faults which they had committed. . . .

I have known a man rejoice so heartily over the struggles and conquests of others, show such pleasure in their progress in virtue that it seemed as though not they but he himself was going to receive the reward of their merits and labours.

I have known a man possess such a burning desire for his neighbours' salvation that he often begged the Divine Goodness with his whole heart, with warm tears and a lofty zeal worthy of Moses, either to grant them salvation or to condemn him too, along with them. For he was bound to them, in the Holy Spirit, with such a saintly love that he was unwilling even to enter the kingdom of heaven, if this should mean he must be separated from them.

SIMEON THE NEW THEOLOGIAN [11]

A certain man gave a great banquet and invited many. (Gospel)

The late medieval pre-occupation with background speculation and the attacks on the Real Presence, powerful and crushing as they were, have blinded us to the things immediately symbolized by the Holy Eucharist. Massive speculations to explain the Real Presence with scientific methods not only deprived the sacrificial aspects of the Mass of their true position in the dogmatic edifice of catechism-trained Catholics, but almost completely eliminated the most obvious foreground fact that in all the visible structure of the Mass we see a sacred banquet, while we recognize not only it, but also its clear reference to sacrifice. In the late Middle Ages tabernacle and monstrance became the center of worship, while the sacrificial meal was given recognition as "also present," but not in a central position. The compelling features of the banquet, the Supper of the Lord and His apostles, are ignored by most of the popular approaches to this mystery. And this mentality continues to prevail: the ideal is, as before, the solitary approach. (Yet the congregation would still have to assemble even if there were enough priests to go from house to house to celebrate Mass for individual families in order to save the members time, money, and discomfort.)

This solitary mentality forgets that the Sacrament was primarily instituted by Our Lord to bring forth *the Church*. This is the point where the Church is most Church, Church experienced and visible. This is the banquet symbolizing Heaven. Until we have learned to see the great significance of this neglected rite—giving hosts from the very same Mass to the gathered Christians—we will be defending causes of the distant past. The Eucharist's first purpose is to build and nourish the Church. As soon as the attitude has changed from individual communion alone to the reintegration of the vaster and richer purpose of this Sacrament, the majority of Catholics will be ready for union. So powerful are the symbols of the Eucharist that, unaided and by themselves, they bear fruit all over the Catholic World. This is clearly noticeable in the rubrics and documents coming from Rome.

Tabernacle-centered worship and adoration of the species were perfectly legitimate when those who are now separated rejected the lasting Presence of the Master. But growing groups who plead for reform within the Protestant communions have by now discovered that they are dealing not with "abominable idolatry," but with a legitimate development that grew out of proportion to the central concern of this Sacrament. In theory, this disproportion was never the official teaching of the Church. Those who spoke for a restriction of the Eucharist to a "Communion of the Eye" were usually men fighting for a cause, especially in the mid-nineteenth century. They had their day and they are gone, but the impact they left on our authors, clergy, religious, seminaries, and lay people is not so easily erased. It will take generations to counter-balance the emphasis into its correct proportion.

H. A. REINHOLD [12]

THE SACRED HEART OF JESUS

(FRIDAY AFTER THE SECOND SUNDAY AFTER PENTECOST)

In the specific forms it has taken in modern times, pious concentration on the heart of Jesus, the symbol of his all-embracing love, stems from the seventeenth-century devotions preached by St. John Eudes and St. Margaret Mary Alacoque. But the remoter origins of the devotion lie in the writings of such outstanding medieval mystics as St. Bonaventure, St. Gertrude, St. Catherine of Siena, Walter Hilton, and others.

The threefold triumph.

Our Saviour has now ascended into heaven, his body bedecked with the splendor of eternal glory; he has taken his throne at the Father's right hand. But he has not ceased to love his spouse, the Church, with that furnace of love wherewith his heart still throbs. On his hands, on his feet, and in his side he bears the glorious marks of his wounds, showing forth his threefold victory over Satan, sin, and death. And in the precious repository of his heart are stored the fruits of that threefold triumph, even the boundless treasures of his merits which he pours out in flowing abundance on redeemed mankind. This is the consoling truth, proclaimed by the apostle to the gentiles, when he says: *Ascending on high, he led captivity captive; he gave gifts to men. . . . He that descended is the same also that ascended above all the heavens, that he might fill all things.* [Eph. 4, 8. 10]

PIUS XII [13]

Devotio.

The tradition of the liturgy and of the writings which it influenced clearly points up the two fundamental aspects of the Sacred Heart devotion.

First of all the worship of *latria* paid by the Church to her Savior is directed to His whole person and in particular to His human heart, this heart of flesh which is hypostatically united to the Person of the Word and is, consequently, both seat and symbol of infinite love—not just the love of a man, but that of the God-Man. This heart is the center and sign of the love of the Word made flesh, of the charity of God in human form.

Secondly, and because of this, the worship rendered to the Sacred Heart is essentially a worship of adoration, as Pius XII told us. Twice, moreover, in his *Haurietis aquas,* the Pope insisted that the heart we adore is the glorious heart of the Lord. Our first duty toward it is not reparation, but adoration of redeeming love, and consecration—that is, the gift of self which ought to be the response to this love. If there is expiation it is because we take a share in His redeeming sacrifice in order to receive its benefits, the sacrifice of Him who alone takes away the sins of the world.

To adore Him is to offer ourselves to Him; this is the purpose of devotion, in the full sense which the word *devotio* had for the ancients and for St. Thomas, and which it retains in the liturgy. Originally in the Latin of classical antiquity *devovere* and *devotio* referred to the act of dedicating someone to the gods of the netherworld. Christianity took over the words to express that interior disposition by which one dedicates, gives, or consecrates himself to God through Jesus Christ.

Naturally, in recent times when the word "devotion" has come to be connected exclusively with those forms of piety which are more or less emotional, the more or less sincere expressions of certain "devout" souls, the word has been stripped of its rich and noble significance. Today we prefer various substitute expressions, such as "gift of self" or "commitment," yet all are summed up in *devotio,* the word Pius XII has continued to use to characterize the worship we owe to the Sacred Heart.

For *devotio* is really worship, and primarily liturgical worship. Further, it is that form of cult which is the practice of the Christian life, whence the expression, *virtutes colere.* The burden and fruits of the mysteries we celebrate must be made to overflow into our daily conduct.

So it is with the devotion to the Sacred Heart. Once we understand it in the light of liturgical tradition and of the contemporary magisterium which comments upon that tradition, we see it does not stop with Jesus' human heart. It plunges us into the depths of love within the Trinity; it confronts every member of the Church with this mystery of faith. In the eyes of the Father, each of them, and all together, constitute only one heart in the Heart of Jesus.

That is why when St. Paul spoke of charity and its manifestations—concrete practical ones, not sentimental—he would so often say that he loved "in the heart of Jesus Christ, *in visceribus Iesu Christi.*" We cannot love except in the Heart of Jesus Christ, for there is no one except Jesus Christ who loves as it is needful to love.

JEAN LECLERQ [14]

The first apparition.

"One day [December 27, 1673] as I was praying before the Most Holy Sacrament and had a little more leisure than usual—normally the tasks I was given did not leave me much time—I was completely invested with the divine presence, so completely that I utterly forgot myself and where I was. I surrendered myself to this divine Spirit and abandoned my heart to the force of his love. He made me lean for a long time on his divine breast, whilst he revealed to me the marvels of his love and the inexplicable secrets of his Sacred Heart, things which he had hitherto always hidden from me and now disclosed for the first time. But he did it in so plain and effective a manner as to leave me no room for doubting it, such were the results that this grace produced in me, who am always afraid of deceiving myself with regard to what I assert to take place in me.

"He said to me: 'My divine Heart is so inflamed with love for men, and for you in particular, that it can no longer contain within itself the flames of its ardent love, and must needs spread them by your means, and manifest itself to men and enrich them with the precious treasures that I will reveal to you. These treasures contain the graces of salvation and sanctification necessary to draw men out of the abyss of perdition, and I have chosen you, as a very abyss of unworthiness and ignorance, for the accom-

35

plishment of this great design, in order that all may be done by me.'

"Then he asked for my heart, which I implored him to take, and having done so, he placed it within his adorable Heart, showing it to me as a little atom being consumed in a glowing furnace; and then withdrawing it thence like a burning flame in the shape of a heart, he replaced it whence he had taken it, saying: 'Behold, my beloved, a precious pledge of my love, which is inserting in your side a tiny spark of its most fiery flames, to serve as your heart and to consume you until your last moment. And as a sign that the great favor I have just done you is not imaginary, but the foundation of all those that I still have to bestow upon you, although I have closed the wound in your side, the pain of it shall ever remain with you; and though hitherto you have adopted the name of my slave, I now give you that of the beloved disciple of my Sacred Heart.' "

Henceforth the first Friday of every month was marked by special proofs of favor but also by searing pain.

ST. MARGARET MARY [15]

THIRD SUNDAY AFTER PENTECOST

Cast all your care upon the Lord; he will sustain you. (Epistle)

Father,
I abandon myself into your hands;
Do with me what you will.
Whatever you may do, I shall always
    thank you.
I am ready for all, I accept all;
Let only your will be done in me,
and in all your creatures;
no more do I wish than this, O Lord.
Into your hands I commend my soul;
I offer it to you with all the love
    of my heart,

For I love you, Lord, and so need
   to give myself,
To surrender myself into your hands
   without reserve,
And with boundless confidence,
For you are my Father.

CHARLES DE FOUCAULD [16]

This man receives sinners! (Gospel)

And had he made them so fearful? Then would Jesus tell them plainly something he had already let them perceive, namely: that the sinner is not only loved, he is even preferred; that it was for him who was lost the Word was made flesh. All Jesus' words, during the last weeks of his life, betrayed this preference for simple hearts, capable of excess. He who was so harsh with the doctors and the Pharisees, allowed himself to unbend with the humble. It was not by humility nor the spirit of sacrifice that he remained in their midst. He preferred them, or rather he hated the world and gave himself to those who were not of the world. Herod, whom he called "that fox," was the only being of whom he spoke with contempt. It was but a game for him to fight the wise men on their own ground; but he cared nothing about reducing the foolish dialecticians to silence! His real joy was to reveal himself to the poor men crushed under their habitual sins and to open under their feet an abyss of mercy and of pardon.

Thus he compared himself to the shepherd of the sheep who abandons ninety-nine to go after the hundredth which is lost; and who brings it back in his arms. In listening to this parable, everyone must have thought: "He is speaking of me . . ." For which one of them had not weighed, with all his fleshy weight, on the sacred shoulders? They had been gathered up, they had been held up and, covered with mud, they had been pressed against that breast. *So shall there be joy in heaven over one sinner that repents, rather than over ninety-nine just.* [Lk. 15, 7]

FRANÇOIS MAURIAC [17]

37

FOURTH SUNDAY AFTER PENTECOST

The eager longing of creation for the revelation of the sons of God. (Epistle)

Christ must be learned as the most profound definition of every human being, a single image among many images, the soul within our soul. In Him all fullness dwells, as St. Paul says, in Him all things hold together, reconciled through the Blood of His Cross. Without Christ, we are like matter without form, persons without identity, the "hollow men" of T. S. Eliot. With Him, we discover both ourselves and our world, penetrating His Death, Resurrection, and Ascension—living the Cross, sharing in His Life, more fully taking captivity "captive" by the fragmentary and momentary triumphs over evil in and around us, triumphs which will explode into the glory of the King of Heaven and earth. The integrity of our personality has its source in Christ, Who contains man as the "firstborn" of every creature, who heals man in Himself, who consummates him in the Divinity. Man indeed begins the task of becoming fully human when he undertakes the full acceptance of Christ, not merely as one among others to be admired or imitated, not merely as a great figure of history, but as God drawing his human life into the mystery of God. It is a simple, literal truth, finally, to say that only He can help us to accept our brother or restore our families, because only He can heal our inner lives.

Union with Christ is begun, continued, consummated in the Church, which extends in time the existence of the Saviour. And within the Church, the Liturgy portrays His great acts; it is a kind of contemporary epiphany of the Son of God to the world. But more than a manifestation of the Lord, the Liturgy is His saving action, the living out of His service of the Father in the members of His Body, the Redemption at work, with all its connotations of adoration, service, and penetration of society. Here are all the phases of the return to God of our world and of all time, here *the eager longing of creation* [Rom. 8, 19] is loud, the Incarnation,

38

the clash with Satan, the Death, Resurrection, Ascension and Advent of the Spirit are made present in mystery. Here Love is personified, the issues explained, perspective given, values established, power communicated.

PHILIP BERRIGAN [18]

The love, the joy which we can and indeed must take in created things, depends entirely on our detachment. As soon as we take them to ourselves, appropriate them, hug them to our hearts, we have stolen them from God. They are no longer His, but our own. And then they are seen in a new light: they are seen in reference to ourselves, as if we were first cause and last end of their existence, as if they had to serve us the way all created things serve God, their Creator. But then we expect the impossible. Just as created things reflect the beauty and goodness of God, so we too avidly seek to find, in our friends and in the things we love, a reflection of our own superior excellence. But we are always disappointed. Our possessions give us the lie. Our friends evade our importunate expectations, embarrassed by the unseemly hunger of a pride which they know they can never satisfy, even though they allow themselves to be consumed by it.

Before a man can taste true joy in all the beautiful things that God has made, he must train the delicate interior sense which enables him to learn the lesson of wisdom which these modest creatures teach those who have ears to hear. They say to us: "You can use me, and God our Father created me that I might be used by you. I am His messenger, sent to tell you the way to Him. I contain a little of His goodness hidden in the depth of my being. But in order to perceive my goodness, you must respect my dignity as a creature of God. If you seek to deflower the pure integrity of my being, and take me to yourself as if I could be fully possessed by you, you will destroy me, and the beauty God has placed in me will vanish out of your hands. Then you will have profited in no way, you will lose me and defile your own soul. But if you respect me, and leave me as I am, and do not seek to seize me with a full and selfish possession, then I will bring you joy: for I will remain what I am, until by God's will I am changed by the service in which you use me. But in being thus changed I will not be destroyed, for use is not destruction. If you use me, my

39

goodness is taken up to the level of your spirit. By using me in your service of God you consecrate me to Him along with yourself. And thus both of us, who were good from the first as creatures of God, help one another to become holy in Him."

THOMAS MERTON [19]

When Christ said to His apostles: *Come follow Me, and I will make you fishers of men* [Mt. 4, 19], He assigned to them a hard task, which they were to perform as "unprofitable servants," no doubt, but at the same time making use of all their talents. The fisherman does not wait for the fish to come, but strives to capture them. While the Christian labors with God, throws out his net into the water "in His name," and works in the "power of the Spirit," he must, nevertheless, yearn for an abundant haul, and must devote to this end the best of himself, his intelligence, imagination and other human endowments. Unquestionably the Christian message must be proclaimed, but this proclamation has to be supplemented by reflection and planned efforts so as to induce others to follow Christ. Truth endeavors to make itself known, and real charity, which must animate the Body of Christ, cannot rest until all men have accepted the spiritual blessings offered by the Redeemer. A mission of proclaiming and persuading is committed to the royal priesthood of the People of God.

The apostolate is the duty of the People as a whole. All the members must foster in their hearts the concerns about which St. Paul speaks: . . . *my daily pressing anxiety, the care of all the Churches! Who is weak, and I am not weak? Who is made to stumble, and I am not inflamed?* [2 Cor. 11, 28–28] There must be a commitment of the whole Body of Christ, and each individual must apply his strength and his resources so that the heavenly Father may be known and glorified in Christian lands of long standing as well as in the missions.

EMILE-JOSEPH DE SMEDT [20]

FIFTH SUNDAY AFTER PENTECOST

Beloved, be all like-minded. (Epistle)

To be a member is to have neither life, being, nor movement, except through the spirit of the body, and for the body.

The separate member, seeing no longer the body to which it belongs, has only a perishing and dying existence. Yet it believes it is a whole, and seeing not the body on which it depends, it believes it depends only on self, and desires to make itself both centre and body. But not having in itself a principle of life, it only goes astray, and is astonished in the uncertainty of its being; perceiving in fact that it is not a body, and still not seeing that it is a member of a body. In short, when it comes to know itself, it has returned as it were to its own home, and loves itself only for the body. It deplores its past wanderings.

It cannot by its nature love any other thing, except for itself and to subject it to self, because each thing loves itself more than all. But in loving the body, it loves itself, because it only exists in it, by it, and for it. . . .

The body loves the hand; and the hand, if it had a will, should love itself in the same way as it is loved by the soul. All love which goes beyond this is unfair. . . .

We love ourselves, because we are members of Jesus Christ. We love Jesus Christ, because He is the body of which we are members. All is one, one is in the other, like the Three Persons.

BLAISE PASCAL [21]

Go first and be reconciled with your brother and then return and present your offering. (Gospel)

When a man gets angry with his brother and swears at him, when he publicly insults or slanders him, he is guilty of murder and forfeits his relation to God. He erects a barrier not only between himself and his brother, but also between himself and God. He

41

no longer has access to him: his sacrifice, worship and prayer are not acceptable in his sight. For the Christian, worship cannot be divorced from the service of the brethren, as it was with the rabbis. If we despise our brother our worship is unreal, and it forfeits every divine promise. When we come before God with hearts full of contempt and unreconciled with our neighbours, we are, both individually and as a congregation, worshipping an idol. So long as we refuse to love and serve our brother and make him an object of contempt and let him harbour a grudge against me or the congregation, our worship and sacrifice will be unacceptable to God. Not just the fact that I am angry, but the fact that there is somebody who has been hurt, damaged and disgraced by me, who "has a cause against me," erects a barrier between me and God. Let us therefore as a Church examine ourselves, and see whether we have not often enough wronged our fellow-men. Let us see whether we have tried to win popularity by falling in with the world's hatred, its contempt and its contumely. For if we do that we are murderers. Let the fellowship of Christ so examine itself to-day and ask whether, at the hour of prayer and worship, any accusing voices intervene and make its prayer vain. Let the fellowship of Christ examine itself and see whether it has given any token of the love of Christ to the victims of the world's contumely and contempt, any token of that love of Christ which seeks to preserve, support and protect life. Otherwise however liturgically correct our services are, and however devout our prayer, however brave our testimony, they will profit us nothing, nay rather, they must needs testify against us that we have as a Church ceased to follow our Lord. God will not be separated from our brother: he wants no honour for himself so long as our brother is dishonoured. God is the Father, the Father of our Lord Jesus Christ, who became the Brother of us all.

DIETRICH BONHOEFFER [22]

SIXTH SUNDAY AFTER PENTECOST

Let us walk in newness of life. (Epistle)

By now I was prepared to face St. Paul's doctrine of Original Sin. I no longer had any illusions about the nature of man. I could see that not only our own civilisation but all the civilisations of the past revealed the same tendency towards corruption. St. Paul now showed me that this was something in the very nature of man; that his nature was corrupted and that the effects of this corruption were inevitable. The history of our own civilisation, its rejection of God, its development of a false science, its materialism, its immorality, was simply the history of all human civilisation. The "world" as such was evil; it was in a state of "sin". Against this St. Paul set a new hope; there was a possibility of another kind of life than that of the world. It was a passage in the first epistle to the Corinthians which first gave me light on this. I remember writing a long letter to Lewis at this time on the text, *As in Adam all die, even so in Christ shall all be made alive.* [1 Cor. 15, 22] I don't know exactly what I said, but I think I saw clearly now that as we all inherit a nature which has the tendency to evil in it, so we may all receive a new nature in Christ. By this I understood that there is an organic unity in mankind; we all inherit the same nature and we all receive the promise of a new nature in Christ. It was then that for the first time the real meaning of the Church dawned on my mind. Until this time I do not think that it had ever been more than a social institution in my eyes. Now I realised that the Church was nothing less than this new humanity. It was a social order indeed, but it was an order that transcended this world, that is to say, all human civilisation. It was a social organism of which Christ was the "head" and all men were potentially its members.

BEDE GRIFFITHS [23]

43

I have compassion on the crowd. (Gospel)

ON ANOTHER'S SORROW

Can I see another's woe,
And not be in sorrow too?
Can I see another's grief,
And not seek for kind relief?

Can I see a falling tear,
And not feel my sorrow's share?
Can a father see his child
Weep, nor be with sorrow fill'd?

Can a mother sit and hear
An infant groan an infant fear?
No, no! never can it be!
Never, never can it be!

And can he who smiles on all
Hear the wren with sorrows small,
Hear the small bird's grief and care,
Hear the woes that infants bear,

And not sit beside the nest,
Pouring pity on their breast;
And not sit the cradle near,
Weeping tear on infant's tear!

And not sit both night and day,
Wiping all our tears away?
O, no! never can it be!
Never, never can it be!

He doth give his joy to all;
He becomes an infant small;
He becomes a man of woe;
He doth feel the sorrow too.

Think not thou canst sigh a sigh
And thy maker is not by;
Think not thou canst weep a tear
And thy maker is not near.

O! he gives to us his joy
That our grief he may destroy;
Till our grief is fled and gone
He doth sit by us and moan.

WILLIAM BLAKE [24]

SEVENTH SUNDAY AFTER PENTECOST

Free from the slavery of sin. (Epistle)

To be free man must love and give himself. Love, which took the deepest wound, receives the most radical healing. For grace is a love that gives itself, and invades the soul to stir up another love unit; grace is *the love of God poured forth in our hearts by the Holy Ghost who is given to us.* [Rom. 5, 5] At the heart of the will, at the source of its energy, there is henceforth the power of divine charity, merited by Christ and given by the Spirit; a gracious "drawing" that manifests the presence of the Father; a profound call, and so sweetly accordant with the natural movement that even while rectifying and passing beyond it, it does but carry it on; the outpouring of a desire, of a gift, of a joy, springing up to life eternal—"living water" as St. Ignatius of Antioch said, "springing within me and murmuring: 'Come to the Father.'" [*Ad Rom.* 7] By changing this man's love grace has changed all his powers, and because his will is now really turned towards his end, its impotence has gone, its deviation is rectified, its egoism is dissolved. It has become an efficacious generosity, and to those thus liberated this counsel can be given: *You, brethren, have been called unto liberty: only make not liberty an occasion to the flesh, but by charity of the spirit serve one another.* [Gal. 5, 13] Love that comes to birth, frail as a new-born babe, enwrapped in all manner of weakness—*infantem pannis involutum*—but des-

45

tined to grow, and to subdue and transform the entire personality. For indeed the Christian who is animated by charity loves God more than himself, he is freed from the egoism that mews him up within himself, from the crippling hardness of heart, the freezing isolation. His heart has become as the heart of a child, open to the evangelical "sweetness," to the compassion that makes all one; he enters into communion with the Father, with his Saviour, with his brothers; he is ready for fellowship, friendship and service. Love that breaks all fetters has set him free. Because it participates in this new love, which is the love of God Himself, the will now knows another inclination, another joy, another hope; it is capable of a new impulsion, a new choice, a new engagement, in short of a new liberty—the liberty of the children of God.

JEAN MOUROUX [25]

By their fruits you will know them. (Gospel)

The way of Christian perfection begins with a personal summons, addressed to the individual Christian by Christ the Lord, through the Holy Spirit. This summons is a call, a "vocation." Every Christian in one way or other receives this vocation from Christ —the call to follow him. Sometimes we imagine that vocation is the prerogative of priests and of religious. It is true that they receive a special call to perfection. They dedicate themselves to the quest for Christian perfection by the use of certain definite means. Yet every Christian is called to follow Christ, to imitate Christ as perfectly as the circumstances of his life permit, and thereby to become a saint.

Our reply to this call of Christ does not consist in saying many prayers, making many novenas, lighting vigil lights before the statues of the saints, or in eating fish on Friday. It does not merely consist in attendance at Mass, or the performance of certain acts of self-denial. All these things may be very good when seen in the full context of the Christian life. Taken out of this context they may be devoid of religious significance, mere empty gestures.

Our response to Christ means taking up our cross, and this in

46

turn means shouldering our responsibility to seek and to do, in all things, the will of the Father. This was, in fact, the whole essence of Christ's own earthly life, and of his death and resurrection. All was done in obedience to the Father. So, too, Christ says to every Christian: *The kingdom of heaven will not give entrance to every man who calls me Master, Master; only to the man who does the will of my Father who is in heaven.* [Mt. 7, 21]

THOMAS MERTON [26]

EIGHTH SUNDAY AFTER PENTECOST

If you live according to the flesh, you shall die. (Epistle)

What Christianity wants is to bring the *whole* person into a living relation to, a movement toward God. In order that he may do this, the bonds which bind him to the world must be broken. And these bonds lie in the will, in servility to the instincts of power, property, and sex. Somehow those shackles must be removed. How, is a question of individual vocation. For the one it means that he must learn to possess properly, and he can learn this only by a practice of self-denial that is really not easy; for another, that he renounce them entirely. For the first, what is demanded is the right use of power over the self and others, and this can be learned only after long schooling in true responsibility and earnest discipline; for the second, renunciation is made possible by absolute obedience. For the first, the answer is marriage based on loyalty and constant discipline of the meandering senses. Christ says also of this solution: understand it who can; for the second, the answer is complete renunciation, and the directing of love's entire strength to God. The two ways of life belong together. They are mutually dependent. Which of them the individual is called to, only his inmost consciousness of vocation can say.

For one called to take the way of renunciation—of powerlessness, propertylessness and loneliness—that way becomes for him no longer one possible form of Christian life among others; it is identical with Christian existence itself. The decision whether he wants to become a genuine Christian, he personally, as God sees

47

and summons him, can reach only through his yes or no. Only blind presumption can speak contemptuously of asceticism. Can such a thing as a dignified human life exist without it—that is, can it without discipline and renunciation exist at all? To say nothing of a life with any degree of greatness? Then how can anyone who takes Christian existence and the Gospel demands seriously possibly deprecate asceticism? It would be incomprehensible—unless of course what is meant by this much-bandied word is something quite different: a technique of intellectual ascent, or some method of painful measures with a view to religious results, in other words, systematic magic. But then it is unfair, in decrying such "ascetic" practices, to accuse Christianity, for Christianity condemns them much more sharply, authoritatively, than does any vague conglomeration of ethical or religious sentiments. It denounces them—for anyone who knows what he is doing—as sin against the Holy Ghost. Everything in its place. We must learn to see how Christian asceticism differs from yoga or from magic of any kind. This means simply that, in the Christian life, faith has consequences, that to "serve God" we must renounce "Mammon," that to be free for God we must break the hold that the world has on us. Faith demands a reconstruction of the inner life, a reforming that can be brought about only by overcoming. That is asceticism.

ROMANO GUARDINI [27]

All who are led by the Spirit of God are the sons of God. (Epistle)

Each time we attempt to force a solution of our difficulties in a quick, easy way we refuse to enter the school of life. This is especially true of the problems of sin and imperfection. Our personal inclinations to certain types of sin and imperfection will be with us as long as we live. They are rooted in our unique nature and in the dark recesses of our past. To be sure, we must try to overcome them in the current of our existence, but we must also humbly accept the fact that possibly we shall never be wholly rid of them in spite of our efforts. It may be that we must live with a certain imperfection to the end of our life; that we must patiently try to cope with it in countless ways while never succeeding in

48

eliminating it. A certain sin may persecute us until our last breath, humiliate us in the eyes of others, escape our understanding, and fill our eyes with tears. This fact we must accept.

The Lord will never ask how successful we were in overcoming a particular vice, sin, or imperfection. He will ask us, "Did you humbly and patiently accept this mystery of iniquity in your life? How did you deal with it? Did you learn from it to be patient and humble? Did it teach you to trust not your own ability but My love? Did it enable you to understand better the mystery of iniquity in the lives of others? Did it give you the most typical characteristic of a truly religious person—that he never judges or condemns the sin and imperfection of others?" The religious man knows from his own life that the demon of evil can be stronger than man even in spite of his best attempts; he knows that it is the patience, humility, and charity learned from this experience that count. Success and failure are accidental. The joy of the Christian is never based on his personal religious success but on the knowledge that his Redeemer lives. The Christian is the man who is constantly aware of his need of salvation. Acceptance of the mystery of iniquity in our project of existence is a school of mildness, mercy, forgiveness, and loving understanding of our neighbor.

ADRIAN VAN KAAM [28]

NINTH SUNDAY AFTER PENTECOST

The people sat down to eat and drink and rose up to play. (Epistle)

When our Blessed Lord describes the days before the Flood, and again those which shall precede the end of the world, He portrays them rather as times of worldliness than of open sin. Men were eating and drinking, marrying and giving in marriage: and He says no more. Now none of these things are wrong in themselves. We can eat and drink, as the apostle teaches us, to the glory of God, and marriage was a divine institution at the time of the Flood, and is now a Christian Sacrament. In the same way when He describes the life of the only person whom the Gospel narra-

49

tive follows into the abode of the lost, He sums it up as the being clothed in purple and fine linen, and feasting sumptuously every day. Here again there is nothing directly sinful in the actions which He names. It surely cannot be a mortal sin to have fine linen, nor will a man lose a state of grace because he feasts sumptuously every day, provided that no other sins follow in the train of this soft life. The malice of it all is in its wordliness, in the fact that this was all or nearly all the lives of those before the flood, of those before the days of anti-Christ, and of the unhappy Dives. Life began and ended in worldliness. There was nothing for God. It was comprised in the pleasures of the world, it rested in them, it was satisfied by them. Its characteristic was sins of omission. Worldliness might almost be defined to be a state of habitual sins of omission. The devil urges men on to great positive breaches of the divine commandments. The passions of the flesh impel sinners to give way to their passions by such dreadful sins, as catch the eyes of men and startle them by their iniquity. Worldliness only leads to these things occasionally and by accident. It neither scandalizes others, nor frightens the sinner himself. This is the very feature of it, which, rightly considered, ought to be so terrifying. The reaction of a great sin, or the shame which follows it, are often the pioneers of grace. They give self-love such a serious shock, that under the influence of it men return to God. Worldliness hides from the soul its real malice, and thus keeps at arm's length from it some of the most persuasive motives to repentance. Thus the Pharisees are depicted in the Gospel as being eminently worldly. It is worldliness, not immorality, which is put before us. There is even much of a moral decency, much of respectable observance, much religious profession; and yet when our Blessed Saviour went among them, they were further from grace than the publicans and sinners. They had implicit hatred of God in their hearts already, which became explicit as soon as they saw Him. The Magdalen, the Samaritan, the woman taken in adultery, —it was these who gathered round Jesus, attracted by His sweetness, and touched by the grace which went out from Him. The Pharisees only grew more cold, more haughty, more self-opinionated, until they ended by the greatest of all sins, the crucifixion of our Lord. For worldliness, when its selfish necessities drive it at last into open sin, for the most part sins more awfully and more impenitently than even the unbridled passions of our nature. So again there was the young man who had great possessions, and who loved Jesus when he saw him, and wished to follow Him. He was a religious man, and with humble scrupulosity observed the commandments of God; but when our Lord told him to sell all and give the price to the poor and to follow Him, he turned away sorrowful, and was found unequal to such a blessed vocation. Now his refusing to sell his property was surely not a mortal sin. It does not appear that our Lord considered him to have sinned by his refusal. It was the operation of worldliness. We do not know what the young man's future was; but a sad cloud of misgivings must hang over the memory of him whom Jesus invited to follow Him, and who turned away. Is he looking now in heaven upon that Face, from whose mild beauty he so sadly turned away on earth?

FREDERICK WILLIAM FABER [29]

My house shall be called a house of prayer. (Gospel)

The Church is not an abstraction; the Church is not merely a worldwide institution founded by Christ to guarantee salvation. The Church as experienced by its members is first of all the local worshiping community, the holy people of God gathered around its ordained minister, for the purpose of discovering each other as brothers in Christ through the united worship of a common Father. It is the Eucharist that makes us brothers. By singing together, by praying with others at Mass, we lie unless our hearts thereby deliberately embrace our neighbor as brother. The liturgical program of active participation is a true worship of God only to the extent that all present unite willingly as his family in one faith and one love.

Self-awareness of the Church entails, therefore, discovering anew the horizontal bond of eucharistic unity by which we become one in Christ, in order that, as a united people, we may address ourselves to our heavenly Father. It means a rediscovery of our dignity as *a chosen race, a holy nation, a purchased people, a holy priesthood to offer spiritual sacrifices acceptable to God through Jesus Christ.* [1 Pet. 2, 9] Self-awareness of the

Church, in its most basic and important sense, means that the parish know itself as the Church in action.

GODFREY DIEKMANN [30]

TENTH SUNDAY AFTER PENTECOST

One Spirit, many gifts.

The Spirit of Christ, the active principle of the entire Church, leads and guides her not only through the hierarchy, from above, but also through the faithful, from below. Both office and charism are essential to the whole of the Church, and both come under the guidance of Christ the Lord. Both are ecclesial. When we look for the way in which the Church is a sign raised up among the nations to show to all the victorious Christ, we must look not only to the teaching authority of the Church and to its pastoral government but also, and as essentially, to the Christian lives of the faithful: to their constancy, as to their unselfish love and goodness, to the humility and faith and resignation with which they bear life's difficulties, to the living Christian example and the responsibility of a father and a mother, to the courage and purity of heart which is visible in their actions, to the virginity of those who consecrate themselves wholly to Christ, to the "old maids" who, though they may not have wanted to remain unmarried, nevertheless do not become soured by their lot but know how to give it the meaningfulness of a new vocation.

All of these are true manifestations of the Church, the visible presence of grace among us. So are the various forms of desire for grace: the appearance among the laity of a variety of Christian movements, of hopes and trends towards new forms of Christian life and activity—in all this the Spirit of Christ is guiding and governing the Church. The works that Christian artists and thinkers achieve through the strength of their life in the eucharistic communion in grace, the forces they release in the context and in the mind of all Christendom—all this is a true part of the reality of the Church, all this is the visible activity of grace among us, a sacrament of God's love for men. In some periods of the Church's history the movements created by Christian writers and thinkers and the results they have produced have done far more to manifest the presence of grace than has the hierarchical government of the Church. . . .

The Spirit of Christ breathes where he will, not only on the Pope and among the ranks of the bishops, but also among the people and their priests. The assistance of the Spirit which Christ has granted to his Church is not only for the exercise of the hierarchical office in the Church, but for the life of the Church in every other aspect too. It is granted to the whole community of believers. True, the whole life of the Church remains under the control of the Church's authority, which is supreme and from which there is no possible appeal. But it is of the essence of the ecclesial character of the hierarchy that it allow the true ecclesial character of the laity its proper scope.

EDWARD SCHILLEBEECKX [31]

Jesus spoke this parable to some who prided themselves on being righteous and despised others. (Gospel)

> The Pharisees want other people to be perfect.
> They insist upon it and demand it, and speak of
> nothing else. But I'm not so demanding.
> Because I know what perfection is, I don't demand
> so much of it from men.
> Because I am perfect, because I alone am perfect.
> I am All-Perfect. I am also less difficult,
> less demanding.
> I am the Holy of Holies.
> I know what holiness is. I know what it costs.
> I know what it costs, I know what it's worth.
> The Pharisees are always calling for perfection,
> For other people. In other people.
> But the saint who want perfection for himself,
> In himself,
> And who searches for it and labors for it in
> pains and tears,

And who sometimes obtains a certain degree of perfection,
The saint is not as difficult as others are.
He makes fewer demands of others. He understands.
He demands a good deal of himself, is hard on
himself. It is a little more difficult than
being hard on others.

CHARLES PEGUY [32]

ELEVENTH SUNDAY AFTER PENTECOST

Christ . . . rose again on the third day. (Epistle)

Our experience of a life that is subject to death continually re-
awakens in us the joy of living and the passionate longing for the
highest and most perfect form of life—for immortality. One person alone succeeded in making this "break-through" to immortality, in the absolute sense. It was Christ, our Pasch. In fellowship
with him, however, we too are enabled to achieve this "break-
through." We achieve it in celebrating the mysteries of our faith,
and in basing our lives on the principles of this new life. That is
no idle dream. It is the reality upon which every man enters at his
Baptism.

We must concern ourselves more and more with this "break-
through" to life. *You know well enough,* says St. Paul, *that we
who were taken up into Christ by baptism have been taken up, all
of us, into his death . . . that so, just as Christ was raised up by
his Father's power from the dead, we too might live and move in
a new kind of existence.* [Rom. 6, 2–4] We should, then, concern
ourselves more and more with this "break-through" to life, valu-
ing the lesser form of life for what it is, that we may win the
highest kind of life, immortal life. How can we fail to be attracted
by a "break-through" such as this? The Christian message of such
a "break-through" ought at least to claim our attention. It is,
after all, a matter of life and death.

In this world of time, there are many ways in which we can
effect this Pasch, this "break-through" to life. We celebrate it li-

turgically in the ceremonies of the Church. We celebrate it, too, by raising up our minds and hearts to God in prayer, for every true prayer is, in a certain sense, a Pasch. We celebrate it by practising Christian asceticism and doing God's will, for this too necessarily involves a certain renunciation of the world. All these acts contribute, to a greater or lesser degree, to our winning through to the ultimate reality of the Pasch, into which we will enter with the crucified and risen Christ, our Pasch, manifestly and humanly comprehensible, in the fullness of life and power, in the wealth and majesty of God's Kingdom. That is the final goal of our Pasch as intended by God. His people of the old and new dispensations will together win through to this final stage of the Pasch in the unity of the one God. Then, too, will be the great Pasch of the entire cosmos, when it breaks through from the transient forms of this world to the external form of the new heaven and new earth.

JOHANNES PINSK [33]

Ephphatha, Be opened! (Gospel)

Since our first parents lent a willing ear to the voice of Satan, we are all deaf to the voice of the eternal Word of God within our souls. And yet we know full well that this divine Word is indescribably close to our souls, closer than our own thoughts, or our very nature to our conscious existence. Within our inmost souls dwells that divine Word, and He addresses us without ceasing. Man hears Him not, for he is afflicted with great deafness. Nor is this a blameless state of deafness, for we are like one to whom something is spoken, and who stops his ears lest he shall hear what it is. We are worse; we have done this so much that at last we have lost knowledge of ourselves, and are become dumb, that is to say, wholly stupid. Ask a worldly man about his interior life, and he is dumb—he knows not if there be any such a life. And the cause of it is that the enemy has crept into that soul, which has hearkened to him, and thus has become deaf and dumb. . . .

And now comes our Lord to a man deaf and dumb, and He spiritually puts His finger in his ears, and anoints his tongue with His holy spital, and immediately the man's soul can hear and can

55

speak. O children, wonderful words might be said of this act of our Lord; we content ourselves with naming the seven gifts of the Holy Ghost, which thus enter the soul and are granted when it hearkens to God in very truth.

First is the spirit of fear, which is given us that we may renounce all self-will, all self-conceit. It teaches us to fly from every evil thing. After that is granted the gift of piety, making us tender-hearted, hindering all rash judgment, rendering us yielding and kindly towards all. The third touch of the Lord's finger is the gift of knowledge, giving us an interior lesson of divine experience, and guiding us to know the inner ways of union with God's holy will. The fourth is divine fortitude, by which the soul is so strengthened as to be able easily to suffer all pain for God's sake, and courageously to undertake all heavy tasks in His honor. The fifth is holy counsel, making all who receive it lovable men, and acceptable guides to others. And now come two touches of the divine finger that are deep and strong, namely, understanding and wisdom; but as to these, one can more easily feel the worth of them than he can describe them. May God grant that our ears may thus be opened to His truth, and that we may ever hearken to His eternal Word. *Amen.*

JOHN TAULER [34]

TWELFTH SUNDAY AFTER PENTECOST

A certain man was going down from Jerusalem to Jericho. [Lk. 10, 30] The use of the specific noun is to the point: not "somebody was going down," but "a certain man"; for the whole of humanity is in question, inasmuch as it has fallen, through the disobedience of Adam, from the height of the abode of Paradise —lofty and calm, passionless and godlike, here aptly called "Jerusalem," which means "peace of God"—to the depth of Jericho, low-lying and stifled in heat—meaning the ardent life of this world, which separates from God and drags down, which causes suffocation in the heat of shameful desire, and chokes to death.

Once humanity had gone astray towards this life, and had lost her balance and been drawn down, borne little by little, to the lowest point of the downward path, as I have said, there settled on her a swarm of savage demons, like a band of brigands; and they

56

stripped her of the cloak of virtue, leaving her not a vestige of fortitude or temperance or justice or prudence, or of anything that represented the image of God; and so they hacked her to death with the repeated wounds of various sins, leaving her cut to pieces; in a word, halfdead. . . .

So while humanity was lying prostrate and all but fainting to death, she was visited by the Mosaic Law; for this is of course the meaning of the priest and the Levite, since it was the Law that taught the Levitic priesthood. It did indeed visit her, but it fell short in competence, and was not equal to a full treatment; it did not even raise the prostrate form, but went perforce, in its incompetence, on an ineffectual round. For sacrifices and gifts were offered through it, as Paul said, which were unable to perfect the worshipper in conscience; because, again, it was impossible that the blood of bulls and goats should entirely take away sin. . . .

At last *a certain Samaritan who was going on a journey came to where he was.* [10, 33] Now it was to the point that Christ here called himself a Samaritan; for since he was dealing with a lawyer, who prided himself greatly on the Law, he took care to show by his words that it was not the priest or the Levite, or indeed, to speak in general terms, those who thought to model their conduct on the Mosaic statutes, but himself who was come to fulfil the will of the Law, and to show by actual practice who was really one's neighbour, and what it was to love him as oneself —he to whom the Jews said as an insult: *You are a Samaritan, and you have a devil.* [Jn. 8, 48] . . .

This Samaritan then, who was going on a journey—that is, Christ—visited the prostrate man. For he had in fact really *come* on the journey; he was not just passing by, as he was making the journey for that very purpose—to visit us, the people for whom he came down to earth and with whom he dwelt. For he did not merely show himself, but also lived among mankind, becoming man in truth, without figure or fancy; for it is distinctive of true and charitable physicians to live among the sick, and not leave them before they are cured. . . . When pouring wine on the wounds—The Word, instructive but pungent, . . . "the wine of repentance"— . . . since . . . the severity . . . of the wounds could not bear a strong astringent, he tempered it with oil. That was why he sat at table with publicans and sinners, and told the

57

contentious Pharisees, when they brought his human kindness against him as a reproach: *Go and learn what this means: It is mercy I want, not sacrifices.* [Mt. 9, 13] Next, he says, he mounted him on a beast; meaning that because "man" as the Scripture says, *when he was well off, did not use his intelligence, but imitated the senseless beast, and became like it* [Ps. 48, 13], and fell sick of every beastly and unclean desire: so Christ, who knew not sin, having become the first-fruits of our race, showed first in himself that having trampled down these beastly passions we have mounted and risen above them; for he has taken the weight of our infirmities and borne the load of our ills. That is why he said that he mounted him, when he had received treatment, on his own beast; for he was bearing us in himself, because we are members of his own body.

But what is more, "he brought him to an inn." Now, πανδοχεῖον —that is, "inn," literally "all-receiving"—is his name for the Church, which has become receptive and holds all mankind: for no longer do we hear, in the restrictive manner of the foreshadowing in the Law and the worship by symbols, *the Ammonite and the Moabite shall not enter the Assembly of the Lord* [Dt. 23, 3], but: *Go and teach all nations* [Mt. 28, 19] and *in every nation, he that fears him and does what is right is acceptable to him.* [Acts 10, 35] And having brought him to the inn, he showed still more solicitude for him. For, indeed, when the Church had been assembled from nations dying of polytheism, Christ himself was in it, dwelling and moving, as the Scripture says, and giving every spiritual grace.

SEVERUS OF ANTIOCH [35]

Let us love God, my dear brothers, let us love God. And let us love until our arms ache and the sweat runs down our faces.

ST. VINCENT DE PAUL [36]

THIRTEENTH SUNDAY AFTER PENTECOST

The promises were made to Abraham and to his posterity. (Epistle)

By faith Abraham received the promise that in his seed were to be blessed all the nations of the earth. Time passed, the possibility remained, Abraham believed: time passed, the possibility became absurd, Abraham believed. There was once a man who also lived in hope. Time passed, the evening of his life drew near; and he was not so mean as to have forgotten his hope, and therefore he shall not be forgotten. Then he sorrowed and his sorrow did not deceive him as life had deceived him, but it gave him all it could, and in the sweetness of sorrow he became possessed of his disappointed hope. It is human to cry out and human to weep among those who are weeping, but it is a greater thing to believe, a more blessed thing to look upon the believer. But Abraham left no song of lamentation. As time passed he did not mournfully count the days: he did not look at Sara wondering suspiciously whether she was growing old: he did not stay the course of the sun to prevent her from ageing, and his hopes with her: he did not lull her with songs of lamentation. Abraham grew old and Sara became a laughing stock to the people, and yet he was God's chosen one, heir to the promise that in his seed were to be blessed all the nations of the earth. Would it not have been better if he had not been the elect of God? What does it mean to be God's elect? It means to be denied in one's youth all the desires of youth and to have them fulfilled after great labour in old age. But Abraham believed and steadfastly lived in hope. If Abraham had hesitated, he would have surrendered his hope. He would have said to God: "So it is perhaps not Thy will that this should come to pass, and therefore I surrender my desire, which was the only one, my blessedness. My soul is upright and I bear Thee no secret malice, because Thou hast denied it to me." He would not have been forgotten, he would have saved many by his example, but he would not have become the father of faith; for it is a great thing to surrender one's desire, but it is a greater thing to abide by it

59

steadfastly after having surrendered it: for it is a great thing to seize the eternal, but a greater thing to abide steadfastly by the temporal after having surrendered it.

There came the fullness of time. If Abraham had not believed, Sara would surely have died of sorrow and Abraham, dulled by grief, would not have understood the fulfilment: he would have smiled at it as a youthful dream. But Abraham believed and therefore he remained young: for he who always hopes for the best becomes old, deceived by life, and he who is always prepared for the worst grows old early, but he who believes preserves eternal youth.

Praised therefore be this story! For Sara, although stricken in years, was still young enough to desire the pleasures of motherhood, and Abraham, although grey-haired, was young enough to desire to be a father. In an external sense the miracle lies in the fact that their wish was fulfilled, but in a deeper sense the miracle of faith lies in the fact that both Abraham and Sara were young enough to wish and that their faith preserved their wish—and with their wish their youth. He received the fulfilment of the promise and he accepted it in faith, and it came to pass according to the promise and to the faith: for Moses struck the rock with his staff, but did not believe.

There was joy in the house of Abraham when Sara became a bride on their golden wedding day.

SØREN KIERKEGAARD [37]

It is above all in the great prayer-act of praise and thanksgiving, the canon of the Mass, that Christians express their gratitude for all the marvels which our heavenly Father has wrought on our behalf. The following selection is from what is probably the earliest recorded eucharistic prayer.

With regard to the eucharist, this is the way you should give thanks. First, for the chalice:

We give you thanks, Father,
for the holy vine of your servant, David,
which you made known to us through Jesus, your Child.
Glory to you throughout the ages.

For the broken bread:
    We give you thanks, Father,
    for the life and knowledge
    you sent us through Jesus, your Child.
    Glory to you throughout the ages.
    As the elements of this broken bread, once scattered
    over the mountains,
    were gathered together and made one,
    so may your Church be built up from the ends of the earth
    and gathered into your kingdom.
    Glory and power are yours
    through Jesus Christ and ever will be. . . .
When you have had your fill, give thanks thus:
    We give you thanks, holy Father,
    for your holy name,
    which you planted in our hearts
    and for the knowledge, faith and immortality
    you sent us through Jesus Christ, your Child.
    Glory to you throughout the ages.
    You created everything, sovereign Lord,
    for the glory of your name.
    You gave food and drink to men
    for their enjoyment,
    as an occasion of thanksgiving;
    and to us you have given the blessing
    of spiritual food and drink
    and eternal life, through your Child.
    Above all we thank you
    because you are powerful.
    Glory to you throughout the ages.
    Remember, Lord, to deliver your Church from all evil
    and to teach it to love you perfectly.
    You have made it holy: build it up from the four winds
    and gather it into the kingdom you destine it for.
    Power and glory are yours
    throughout the ages.
    Come grace and the world may pass on its way.
    Hosannah to the God of David.
    If you are holy, come forward;

if you are not, repent.
Maranatha.
Amen.

THE DIDACHE [38]

FOURTEENTH SUNDAY AFTER PENTECOST

The fruits of the spirit are . . . (Epistle)

If there is righteousness in the heart,
There will be beauty in the character.

If there is beauty in the character,
There will be harmony in the home.

If there is harmony in the home,
There will be order in the nation.

When there is order in the nation,
There will be peace in the world.

CHINESE PROVERB [39]

No man can serve two masters. (Gospel)

Two cities have been formed by two loves: the earthly by the love
of self, even to the contempt of God; the heavenly by the love of
God, even to the contempt of self. The former, in a word, glories
in itself, the latter in the Lord. For the one seeks glory from men;
but the greatest glory of the other is God, the witness of conscience. The one lifts up its head in its own glory; the other says
to its God, *You are my glory, and the lifter up of mine head.* [Ps.
3, 4] In the one, the princes and the nations it subdues are ruled
by the love of ruling; in the other, the princes and the subjects
serve one another in love, the latter obeying, while the former
take thought for all. The one delights in its own strength, represented in the persons of its rulers; the others says to its God, *I*

will love you, O Lord, my strength. [Ps. *17, 1*] And therefore the wise men of the one city, living according to man, have sought for profit to their own bodies or souls, or both, and those who have known God *glorified Him not as God, neither were thankful, but became vain in their imaginations, and their foolish heart was darkened; professing themselves to be wise*—that is, glorying in their own wisdom, and being possessed by pride—*they became fools, and changed the glory of the incorruptible God into an image made like to corruptible man, and to birds, and four-footed beasts, and creeping things.* For they were either leaders or followers of the people in adoring images, *and worshipped and served the creature more than the Creator, who is blessed for ever.* [Rom. 1, 21–25] But in the other city there is no human wisdom, but only godliness, which offers due worship to the true God, and looks for its reward in the society of the saints, of holy angels as well as holy men, *that God may be all in all.* [1 Cor. 15, 28]

ST. AUGUSTINE [40]

FIFTEENTH SUNDAY AFTER PENTECOST

He who sows in the flesh shall reap corruption. (Epistle)

Does she groan and lament who has time to put on the clothing of precious apparel, and not to consider the robe of Christ which she has lost; to receive valuable ornaments and richly wrought necklaces, and not to bewail the loss of divine and heavenly ornament? Although you clothe yourself in foreign garments and silken robes, you are naked; although you adorn yourself to excess both in pearls, and gems, and gold, yet without the adornment of Christ you are unsightly. And you who stain your hair, now at least cease in the midst of sorrows; and you who paint the edges of your eyes with a line drawn around them of black powder, now at least wash your eyes with tears. If you had lost any dear one of your friends by the death incident to mortality, you would groan grievously, and weep with disordered countenance, with changed dress, with neglected hair, with clouded face, with

63

dejected appearance, you would show the signs of grief. Miserable creature, you have lost your soul; spiritually dead here, you are continuing to live to yourself, and although yourself walking about, you have begun to carry your own death with you.

ST. CYPRIAN [41]

Young man, arise! (Gospel)

In this complex and continuing reality which is the incarnation of the Word, the climactic event, to which all else looked forward and to which his intercession now looks back, is his death-leading-to-resurrection. In this death his life of obedient, self-dispossessing love was summed up and found its most complete creaturely human embodiment. In this death, too, the Father's redeeming love for mankind found its unsurpassable expression, for we see it mirrored in Christ's love, even unto death, for all the lost and straying brethren whom the Father had given him. Because death was here dominated by love, it led to life for Christ and for the brethren whom he had identified with himself. The power of that death-embracing and death-conquering love, which is a permanent reality in the risen Christ, touches us in every sacrament and gives us the life that was and is in him. We may never, in our enthusiasm for the risen and victorious Christ, forget the earthly life and death of Christ. For it is by his wounds that we are healed, and the life he gives us is indeed the life of the risen Christ, but we possess it in that seminal stage, so to speak, in which he himself possessed it during his earthly life until the resurrection.

In each sacrament the passion and death of Christ heals and enlivens us. Not, however, as though the rest of his earthly life were meaningless for us. Far from it. But his life was all of a piece. It was the one progressive embodiment, in the flesh and blood of the incarnate Word, of God's redemptive will, reflected in and answered by the loving obedience of the Son and Head of the fallen race. In his death we see the climax and clearest manifestation of his rejection of sin and his filial love, of his witness to the Father, of his love for his future Church, of his servantship for men, of his acceptance of death as the paradoxical way to

64

fulness of life in God. In a word, we see reflected in his dying the
life which reveals its various facets to us in the sacraments: one
life, but inexhaustible in its virtualities.

MATTHEW J. O'CONNELL [42]

SIXTEENTH SUNDAY AFTER PENTECOST

He who humbles himself shall be exalted. (Gospel)

That there is a virtue of humility is due to Christ. It has been said
of humility that it is "the sign of Christianity," its characteristic
mark, which presupposes that it must first be the sign of Christ.
And indeed he did say: *Learn of me, because I am meek and
humble of heart.* [Mt. 11, 29]

If a Christian looks for motives of humility, he will find two.
The first comes from his creaturely condition, which places him
wholly in God's power. In this, man's humility is a glory; it is the
recognition of dependence that makes man great. For he is created, he is a man, he is a son of God through this dependence.
The second motive comes from his sinful condition, which places
him even below the creaturely condition: this is the humility of
poverty, the recognition of debasement.

Christ's humility presents two similar aspects. It is founded
upon his condition as man, Son of God, wholly dependent upon
God. But in its other aspect, it relates to sin. In order to save
sinners, he accepted the condition of sinful man which made him
lower than he was, just as sin makes us something less than ourselves. In its first aspect this humility is natural, a humility of
greatness, born of Christ's divine exaltation in his human being.
The other aspect is not a humility of Christ's nature, but of his
redeeming function, a humility which was on earth a humili-
ation. . . .

We can help ourselves along the way to humility by meditating
upon the majesty of God and the nothingness of all created being.
But to seek humility by this road is fraught with dangers. God's
countenance may seem so terrifying that we cannot bear its
splendour; if so, man must simply cast himself face down on the

ground in fear, and may well fall into pusillanimity. It is not for the Christian to lie prostrate and motionless before God; through the pasch of Christ in which he communicates, he must "go to the Father." Any merely intellectual way to humility is bound to remain lifeless and to fail of its effect. Humility is a virtue of the heart filled with the charity of the spirit, and the Spirit *is the truth* [1 Jn. 5, 6] and cannot fail. To be humble, what is essential is to live in the love of God who is in Christ Jesus.

The surest road to humility is Christ. For he is *the way.* [Jn. 14, 6]. The Christian soaks up humility as a sponge soaks up water, if he lives in Christ. After the poverty of earthly man, trying to be a god by closing himself in upon his own littleness, becoming a god only in reverse, there has now come the man from heaven, Jesus, the Lord of humility, in the glory of his openness to God. Born into the pride of Adam, we are begotten to humility as well as to divine life in our Lord Jesus Christ. It is because he has become our way to humility that he is our Saviour. If we did not accept Christ's humility within us, we should have no part in salvation: *If I wash not your feet, you shall have no part with me.* [Jn. 13, 88]

To make certain of a Christianity of union and humility, St. Paul simply urged that we live intensively in Christ: *Let this mind be in you which was also in Christ Jesus, who . . . emptied himself . . . , humbled himself.* [Phil. 2, 7] To be humble, one need only live by Christ. There will gradually cease to be any least trace of pride in those who live only by Christ. Theirs will be a branch on which only humility and charity blossom: "I know that you are not swollen with pride, for you have Christ Jesus in you." [St. Ignatius of Antioch, *Magn.* 12]

F. X. DURRWELL [43]

Humble patience.

The best support for faith is the guarantee that if we ask our Father for bread, he does not give us a stone. Quite apart from explicit religious belief, every time that a human being succeeds in making an effort of attention with the sole idea of increasing his grasp of truth, he acquires a greater aptitude for grasping it, even if his effort produces no visible fruit. An Eskimo story explains the origin of light as follows: "In the eternal darkness, the crow, unable to find any food, longed for light, and the earth was illumined." If there is a real desire, if the thing desired is really light, the desire for light produces it. There is a real desire when there is an effort of attention. It is really light that is desired if all other incentives are absent. Even if our efforts of attention seem for years to be producing no result, one day a light that is in exact proportion to them will flood the soul. Every effort adds a little gold to a treasure no power on earth can take away. The useless efforts made by the Curé d'Ars, for long and painful years, in his attempt to learn Latin bore fruit in the marvelous discernment that enabled him to see the very soul of his penitents behind their words and even their silences.

SIMONE WEIL [44]

SEVENTEENTH SUNDAY AFTER PENTECOST

One Lord, one faith, one baptism. (Epistle)

The liturgy is the summit toward which the activity of the Church is directed; at the same time it is the fount from which all her power flows. For the aim and object of apostolic works is that all who are made sons of God by faith and baptism should come together to praise God in the midst of his Church, to take part in the sacrifice, and to eat the Lord's Supper.

The liturgy in its turn moves the faithful, filled with "the paschal sacraments," to be one in holiness; it prays that they may hold fast in their lives to what they have grasped by their faith; the renewal in the eucharist of the covenant between the Lord and man draws the faithful into the compelling love of Christ and sets them on fire. From the liturgy, therefore, and especially from the eucharist, as from a fount, grace is poured forth upon us; and the sanctification of men in Christ and the glorification of God, to which all other activities of the Church are directed as towards their end, is achieved in the most efficacious possible way.

CONSTITUTION ON THE SACRED LITURGY [45]

Love of God.

Man is the most perfect work of the creation; the soul is the most perfect part of man; the perfection of the soul is love, and that of love is the love of God; which on this account is the end and perfection of the universe. In this consists the pre-eminence of the precept we treat of, which our Lord calls the first and greatest commandment—it may be considered as a sun placed in the middle of the spiritual world, imparting light and motion to the laws of God and works of piety.

Divine love is the end for which everything has been made; all things refer to this virtue. It may be compared to a sacred tree; the commandments of God, his counsels, exhortations, and inspirations are its flowers; eternal life its fruit. As there is no medium between life and death, everything which cannot be referred to this love, which is eternal life, extends to eternal death. We cannot hesitate in allowing that this commandment deserves to be called great; since the practice of it is continued and perfected in heaven, where we shall live eternally, and live only by love.

ST. FRANCIS DE SALES [46]

Love of neighbor.

God, who has created man to his own image, commands us to love all men with a love similar to that which should inflame our hearts for his divine Majesty. *You shall love the Lord your God with your whole heart. This the greatest and first commandment. And the second is like to this: You shall love your neighbor as yourself.* [Mt. 22, 37–39] Why do we love God? St. Bernard replies, that the motive of this love is God himself, thereby insinuating that we love God because he is the sovereign and infinite goodness. But why do we love ourselves with a love of charity? Because we are the image and likeness of God. The dignity of resembling the Almighty is common to all men; we should then love them all as ourselves, that is, as living images of the Deity.

It is on this title that we belong to God; it is this which forms the strict alliance we have contracted with him, and that bond of dependence by which we have become the children of God, who assumes the tender name of a parent in our regard. It is as images of God that we are capable of being united to his divine essence, of enjoying his sovereign goodness, and of being happy with the bliss of God himself. It is in this quality that grace is communicated to us, that our soul is closely united with that of God, and that, according to the expression of St. Leo, we participate in some degree in the divine nature.

The acts of the love of God and our neighbour both proceed from the same charity. One end of the ladder seen by Jacob touched the heavens, and the other rested on the earth, as if to enable the angels to descend, and man to ascend. Thus the same love extends to God and our neighbor; by it we are elevated to union with the Divinity, and we descend to man, to live in union with him; yet by this love we always consider our neighbor as created to the image of God, and thereby communicating with the goodness of God, participating in his graces, and destined to enjoy his glory. Whence it follows, that to love our neighbor with a love of charity, is to love God in man, or man in God, and, consequently, to love God alone for his own sake, and creatures for the love of God.

ST. FRANCIS DE SALES [47]

EMBER DAYS OF SEPTEMBER

In the liturgy of the September ember days are echoes and re-echoes of the ancient Jewish solemnities of the "seventh month," especially of the Day of the Atonement on the tenth, when the high priest entered the holy of holies with the blood of sacrificial victims while the people fasted and prayed in the outer courts. It also commemorated the feast of Tabernacles, a joyous harvest festival of thanksgiving for God's bounty and for his rescuing care. The Gospel readings of all three days recall the profound faith which the Church has in prayer and fasting to expel demons (Wednesday), remit sin (Friday), to stir up the minds and hearts of the faithful, and to free them from their infirmities (Saturday).

69

The Christian life . . . is summed up in prayer. I consider that prayer is the most important and necessary means of salvation and the first duty of every Christian. Prayer is the first step in the devout life and also its crown, and that is why the Gospel bids unceasing prayer. To other acts of piety their own times are assigned, but in the matter of prayer there are no off times. Without prayer it is impossible to do any good and without the Gospel you cannot learn properly about prayer. Therefore, all those who have reached salvation by way of the interior life, the holy preachers of the Word of God, as well as hermits and recluses, and indeed all God-fearing Christians, were taught by their unfailing and constant occupation with the depths of God's Word and by reading the Gospel. Many of them had the Gospel constantly in their hands, and in their teaching about salvation gave the advice: "Sit down in the silence of your cell and read the Gospel and read it again."

THE WAY OF A PILGRIM [48]

I think it can be maintained without falling into an excess of exaggeration that our modern disaffection for fasting as a properly religious exercise reposes on two erroneous conceptions which, paradoxically enough, would appear at first sight to be mutually exclusive.

The first is a kind of vague, Rousseauist naturalism that considers the body to be a good thing in itself which it is unreasonable to treat severely by fasting or other hard using. The second conception would seem to err by a too pronouncedly spiritualist tendency, giving all its attention to the soul and leaving the humble body altogether on one side. This second view of things would see in the body little more than an unimportant envelope to the soul destined to be given over to corruption after death.

Both these ideas are, I believe, widely held and often enough simultaneously held, among perfectly sincere Christians, and yet both are false, because they ignore the true nature of man and his final destiny in God's plan.

If man has sinned and if men go on sinning, their sin is not something which is confined to the mystic recesses of their souls. The grosser and commoner sins positively need the body for their accomplishment. Not only is that true, but the most subtle and

70

immaterial sins also need the help of certain of the nobler functions of the body to come to their effect: the imagination cannot act without the cooperation of the brain, and so forth, so that we can say that the soul sins in and with and by the body and the body sins under the direction of the soul. If the body sins, then it is immediately obvious that the body also needs to be redeemed from sin.

As for the second error, its falsehood is at once shown up by our belief in "the resurrection of the body and life everlasting." Holding these two Christian truths—the body's need of redemption and its calling to share in the heavenly glory—we can at once begin to glimpse some further riches hidden in Christ's gift of the Eucharist and in the Church's traditional practice of fasting before the reception of holy Communion. . . .

Since the fall of our first parents, the body (like the soul) is no longer something wholly good, perfect, pure and well-ordered in itself. Quite apart from that education and training and exercise which it would no doubt have needed in the process of growing from babyhood to manhood even had there been no sin, it now, as fallen man's body, needs in addition correction and chastening.

This correction and chastening are called in common parlance, fasting. Not that fasting is the only effective means of keeping the body in its proper place and function (or more often, or restoring it to these, if it should have proved too restive and disobedient); but it is the chief and most effective means.

GREGORY BAINBRIDGE [49]

EIGHTEENTH SUNDAY AFTER PENTECOST

The day of the coming of our Lord Jesus Christ. (Epistle)

Where are those who rejoice when He comes into their lives; where above all, are those who rejoice to bring nearer the hour of His coming into souls who do not know Him, and who wish to prepare His way before Him, in the continents which are still without the Faith. The Propagation of the Faith should be our perpetual solicitude, the chief of our desires and the cause of our

71

joy. How many are there among us whom this anxiety, at times, prevents from sleeping? When we are expecting news, when we watch for the arrival of a friend, we do not sleep. Evening comes down, night falls, but at the window-sill the watcher listens, facing the stars. Are there many among us, who thus in the silence lie in wait for the stealthy steps of the Redeemer, as He descends by our terrestrial roads towards the sheep of His fold?

We have installed ourselves in a very fairly comfortable life and the delays of the Second Coming can be prolonged without causing us inconvenience. This "Valley of Tears!" we have worked to make as smiling a valley as possible, and it is in spite of us that suffering still lingers there. If we were told that in place of that heaven which is to come we were to be allowed to remain for ever on earth, and that we had permission to make ourselves a nest here, I imagine that many among us would joyfully take part in that adventure, regretting only that they could not, in addition, bring down heaven itself here below. The arrival of Christ is joyful tidings only to the pure of heart. But the further my life advances the more I see that it is covered with spots and, as it were, striped with faults; this ordinary life of a weak and indolent man, without much consistency, more rich in floating illusions than in solid worth, quick to assume that his desires are his actions, and his self-esteem his real value. It is all this falsehood that keeps us far from Christ, that prevents us from longing ardently for His arrival, and from exulting when we are assured that at no distant date we shall meet Him.

Our first fathers in the faith, O Lord, watched for You as for the dawn. You will come at the end of time, in Your own hour, when You choose and when all is ready for the last judgment. What have You still to put into my hands and in what will my eternal lot consist. You must grant me my pardon . . . this pardon given by You! I shall remain upon my knees in the invisible sanctuary, until I have obtained this pardon, just as those to be ordained are commanded not to leave the Church, where they are being consecrated, until the Mass is finished and they have received the blessing of the bishop. . . . You will grant me my forgiveness and also my perseverance, that supreme gift, which You hide as a pearl beneath the bitterness of death, the liberating seal of Your predestined ones. I await it, I must prepare myself more fully for it and live in this blessed expectation—*corde suspenso*. My God, in view of Your final coming, cut down in me all that hinders Your work, break all that serves as a screen, and triumph over all that checks You. Come in Your hour, as a master long desired.

PIERRE CHARLES [50]

Your sins are forgiven. (Gospel)

Lord Jesus Christ, I have heard your word of forgiveness in the Sacrament. I have heard once again what we cannot hear too often: that you will be merciful and forgive me. Time and time again. With inexhaustible patience, forbearingly and faithfully. I thank you for your goodness, for the magnanimity and patience which you have shown me all the days of my life. In this sacrament I experience your grace again and again. I receive your forgiveness, freely granted, to meet my daily need. I need your grace and love again and again in the confessional; grant that I may bring the message of that grace and love to my neighbour in his need. Grant too that I may share his burden by my prayers; that I may be patient and knowing, humble and wise, an apostle, preaching your word so that it may penetrate and convert all hearts. Count me with those who receive and hand on the peace of your forgiveness. May the merciful judgement of your grace, which I receive in the Sacrament of Penance, forever be a promise of that judgement which I am to meet, of the Last Judgement, which will conclude and fulfil all the judgments of this time, both in the sacrament and in our lives.

I am already approaching this judgment. *It is appointed unto men once to die, and after this the judgment.* [Heb. 9, 27] How near, O Lord, am I already to that day; how very near to the moment when I will be parted from all that I do not wish to part from, the moment which comes but once and which we must face alone. Only for three hours do I hang beside you, as a poor thief, on the cross of this world and this age: a short life. Shall I have used it to say to you: Lord, remember me when you come into your kingdom? Shall I have used it, this fleeting moment that I call my life, to put my poor soul into your Father's hand, freely, in faith and love? Shall I have acted in such a way that the words: *It is a fearful thing to fall into the hands of the living God* [Heb. 10, 31] will not refer to me? Lord, when you come like a thief in the night, do not judge me. I do not know when you are coming, I only know that you will come soon. When you come, come in the gentle secrecy of your grace before you come as a judge. Kindle and leave burning in my heart the light of faith and the fire of your love. Before you come as judge, prepare for me the house of my eternity, in which you will live, and see that it is in order and worthy to become my only heaven and yours.

Give me the grace of perseverance. This is what you give, when you give me the grace of unwavering trust in your mercy, when you give me the grace to believe that you are greater than our hearts, when you give me the grace of prayer and of love. You give me the grace of perseverance, in giving me the grace to forget my own wilfulness in the holy mission which you have entrusted to me, in the holy destiny to which you have called me. You give it to me in the grace to love and honour your Sacred Heart and your mother and mine.

KARL RAHNER [51]

NINETEENTH SUNDAY AFTER PENTECOST

Put on the new man. (Epistle)

If any man is in Christ, he is a new creature. [2 Cor. 5, 17] To prevent us from interpreting the text as applying to a visible creation, he stated: *If any man is in Christ,* teaching us that if any man has gone over to the side of those who believe in Christ, he is an example of a new creature. Tell me, if we see new heavens and other portions of His creation, is there a profit in this which can match the benefit we gain from seeing a man converted from evil to virtue and changing from the side of error to that of truth? This is what the blessed Paul called a new creature, and so straightway he went on to say: *The former things have passed away; behold, they are all made new!* [2 Cor. 5, 17] By this he showed in brief that those who, by their faith in Christ, had put

74

off like an old cloak the burden of their sins, those who had been
set free from their error and been illumined by the light of justifi-
cation, had put on this new and shining cloak, this royal robe.
This is why he said: *If any man is in Christ, he is a new creature:
the former things have passed away; behold, they are all made
new.*

ST. JOHN CHRYSOSTOM [52]

Why have you come in here without a wedding garment? (Gospel)

In the Gospels we are told of a man, once, who pushed his way
into a wedding party; how, wearing unsuitable clothes, he went
in, took a place, and ate, since the bridegroom let him do so.
Now when he saw that all were in their brightest clothes, he
ought to have changed into his. But in his appearance and by his
attitude, he was an odd man out, although he was quite one of
the party where the food was concerned. The bridegroom, for his
part, though bountiful, was not undiscerning; and as he went
round the party, giving his attention to each in turn (not, of
course, with any thought what they were eating, but simply of
their nice manners), he came upon this complete stranger not
dressed for the occasion. So he said to him, "Friend, how camest
thou in hither? I mean, in those filthy clothes? Where was your
conscience? Granted that, as the host is lavish, the porter did not
stop you coming in: granted that, when you entered you did not
know what sort of clothes the party demanded: you came in and
saw people at table in brilliant costume: ought you not to have
been put right by what you saw? Should you not have taken your
chance to withdraw and come back suitably dressed? Well, now,
you came in unceremoniously for us to throw you out unceremoniously." So the bridegroom orders the servants, "Bind his feet,
which had the hardihood to bring him in here. Bind his hands,
that could not dress him properly. And throw him out into the
darkness outside, for he does not deserve wedding lights."

ST. CYRIL OF JERUSALEM [53]

75

Grace and new life in Christ.

Very often we think of grace in a static way, almost as a sort of fluid poured into the soul as into a vessel when we receive the sacraments. It is indeed a quality inherent in the soul, but it is at the same time a dynamic force that penetrates and changes our being and then impels us onward in a movement of loving return to the Father. Moreover, we must remember that created grace does not stand by itself as the sufficient explanation of our new existence as sons of God. It raises us to the divine life only because it is a unitive reality which serves as a bond or link establishing our union with the Holy Spirit, who comes to us by grace, unites us to Christ, relates us in Christ to the Father as our Father and moves us in Christ towards the Father in a movement that will only reach its completion in our beatitude and glorious resurrection. The reception and increase of grace must not be thought of as the passive reception of an inert gift. What happens is that we are swept up into a movement that transfers us from the order and dynamism of this world into the order of the Resurrection and the dynamism of the Spirit. Consequently, our reception of grace is the taking place in us of that same process which, considered in its full corporate universality, we call the history of salvation, and, considered in Christ, constitutes the mystery of his redemptive work.

CHARLES DAVIS [54]

TWENTIETH SUNDAY AFTER PENTECOST

Singing and making melody in your hearts to the Lord. (Epistle)

It is said that Paganism is a religion of joy and Christianity of sorrow; it would be just as easy to prove that Paganism is pure sorrow and Christianity pure joy. Such conflicts mean nothing and lead nowhere. Everything human must have in it both joy and sorrow; the only matter of interest is the manner in which the two things are balanced or divided. And the really interesting thing is this, that the pagan was (in the main) happier and happier as he approached the earth, but sadder and sadder as he approached the heavens. The gaiety of the best Paganism, as in the playfulness of Catullus or Theocritus, is, indeed, an eternal gaiety never to be forgotten by a grateful humanity. But it is all a gaiety about the facts of life, not about its origin. To the pagan the small things are as sweet as the small brooks breaking out of the mountain; but the broad things are as bitter as the sea. When the pagan looks at the very core of the cosmos he is struck cold. Behind the gods, who are merely despotic, sit the fates, who are deadly. Nay, the fates are worse than deadly; they are dead. And when the rationalists say that the ancient world was more enlightened than the Christian, from their point of view they are right. For when they say "enlightened" they mean darkened with incurable despair. It is profoundly true that the ancient world was more modern than the Christian. The common bond is in the fact that ancients and moderns have both been miserable about existence, about everything, while mediaevals were happy about that at least. I freely grant that the pagans, like the moderns, were only miserable about everything—they were quite jolly about everything else. I concede that the Christians of the Middle Ages were only at peace about everything—they were quite jolly about everything else. But if the question turn on the primary pivot of the cosmos, then there was more cosmic contentment in the narrow and bloody streets of Florence than in the theatre of Athens or the open garden of Epicurus. Giotto lived in a gloomier town than Euripides, but he lived in a gayer universe.

The mass of men have been forced to be gay about the little things, but sad about the big ones. Nevertheless (I offer my last dogma defiantly) it is not native to man to be so. Man is more himself, man is more manlike, when joy is the fundamental thing in him, and grief the superficial. Melancholy should be an innocent interlude, a tender and fugitive frame of mind; praise should be the permanent pulsation of the soul. Pessimism is at best an emotional half-holiday; joy is the uproarious labour by which all things live. Yet according to the apparent estate of man as seen by the pagan or the agnostic, this primal need of human nature can never be fulfilled. Joy ought to be expansive; but for the agnostic it must be contracted, it must cling to one corner of the world. Grief ought to be a concentration; but for the agnostic its desolation is spread through an unthinkable eternity. This is what I call being born upside down. The skeptic may truly be said to be topsy-turvy; for his feet are dancing upward in idle ecstacies, while his brain is in the abyss. To the modern man the heavens are actually below the earth. The explanation is simple; he is standing on his head; which is a weak pedestal to stand on. But when he had found his feet again he knows it. Christianity satisfies suddenly and perfectly man's ancestral instinct for being the right way up; satisfies it supremely in this; that by its creed joy becomes something gigantic and sadness something special and small. The vault above us is not deaf because the universe is an idiot; the silence is not the heartless silence of an endless and aimless world. Rather the silence around us is a small and pitiful stillness like the prompt stillness in a sick-room. We are perhaps permitted tragedy as a sort of merciful comedy: because the frantic energy of divine things would knock us down like a drunken farce. We can take our own tears more lightly than we could take the tremendous levities of the angels. So we sit perhaps in a starry chamber of silence, while the laughter of the heavens is too loud for us to hear.

Joy, which was the small publicity of the pagan, is the gigantic secret of the Christian. And as I close this chaotic volume I open again the strange small book from which all Christianity came; and I am again haunted by a kind of confirmation. The tremendous figure which fills the Gospels towers in this respect, as in every other, above all the thinkers who ever thought themselves tall. His pathos was natural, almost casual. The Stoics, ancient and modern, were proud of concealing their tears. He never concealed His tears; He showed them plainly on His open face at any daily sight, such as the far sight of His beloved city. Yet He concealed something. Solemn supermen and imperial diplomatists are proud of restraining their anger. He never restrained His anger. He flung furniture down the front steps of the Temple, and asked men how they expected to escape the damnation of Hell. Yet He restrained something. I say it with reverence; there was in that shattering personality a thread that must be called shyness. There was something that He hid from all men when He went up to a mountain to pray. There was something that He covered constantly by abrupt silence or impetuous isolation. There was some one thing that was too great for God to show us when He walked upon our earth; and I have sometimes fancied that it was His mirth.

G. K. CHESTERTON [55]

In Scripture, it is He for whom we must look, Who turns towards us His mysterious Face. How often we have experienced this as we pondered, in the Missal, passages of Scripture of which we could make very little, whose literal meaning escaped us. Our heart was set on fire by a mysterious encounter. Scripture is a person, Scripture is Jesus. Before as after His advent it is full of Him. Before, it is the night drawing towards the dawn; after, it is the sky brilliant with the midday sun. That is why the piety of Christians has always felt so perfectly at ease in the Old Testament, of which every episode is a window resplendent with the brightness of a single luminary, every page part of a dynamic whole, moving towards Christ.

For this reason also we still chant the psalms, several of which express a Messianic hope so exceeded by its realisation that it would be meaningless to recite them to-day if the light of the Spirit did not reveal beyond the words the reference to Christ.

It is the same always. Scripture can be understood only on our knees, as we feed upon it and become aware of an invisible current of air that moves all its leaves in an unconstrainable aspiration towards the glorious Countenance of Jesus Christ. The true sense of Scripture always lies beyond, beyond the words, the concepts, and the events which are but signs in which faith detects the presence of the *Only Son*.

But for this very reason, the sacred texts invite the musical development which will make all that is unutterable in them an audible undertone. It was, therefore, a natural development when in the Liturgy they put on a garb of song; and music sought to render the Divine atmosphere with which the words are invested.

Beyond question, psalmody represents the most remarkable of these efforts. It has discovered the secret of opening words without dispersing their spirit, of weaving a sequence of sounds without violating silence, of withdrawing the soul within herself on a most personal prayer while at the same time uniting her to the

79

souls of others in a public prayer, and providing man with the most moving expression of his needs, a supplication which rises above them and crowns with praise the unutterable groans of the Spirit. Nothing is humbler and simpler, more sublime and more spontaneous, more dynamic and more contemplative. There is no *tour de force*, no excitement, not the least attempt at effect, no glance back at self. It is understood that God can never be expressed and that the important matter is to let Him *utter Himself* in the depths of silence, where His Word is engendered.

That is why psalmody *listens* even more than it sings. The body moreover has its share in this work of praise. It is a part which elevates without exciting it, occupies it without distracting it, and rests it without relaxing it. But while the voice follows the words it sings, the soul surrenders herself to the Spirit. And God alone knows what these contacts may achieve.

The seeming monotony of the Chant still further accentuates the inwardness of the tone, the supreme reserve of faith, and the Divine modesty of love.

Psalmody is, in the sublimest sense of the term, a spiritual music, an interior music at once human and Divine, contemplative and mystical, an act performed in the sphere of the Eucharist and inseparable from it, a sacrament by which Christ prays in the Church for His Father's glory and the salvation of the world.

MAURICE ZUNDEL [56]

TWENTY-FIRST SUNDAY AFTER PENTECOST

Take up the armor of God. (Epistle)

Let us take courage and strip ourselves for the contests. Christ has put on us armor that is more glittering than any gold, stronger than any steel, hotter and more violent than any fire, and lighter than any breath of air. The nature of this armor does not burden and bend our knees, (but it gives wings to our limbs and lifts them up. If you wish to take flight to heaven, this armor is no hindrance. It is a new kind of armor,) since it is a new kind of combat. Although I am a man, I must aim my blows at demons;

although clad in flesh, my struggle is with incorporeal powers. On this account God has made my breastplate not from metal but from justice; He has prepared for me a shield which is made not of bronze but of faith. I have, too, a sharp sword, the sword of the Spirit. The devil shoots darts at me, but I have a sword; he is an archer, but I am a heavy-armed soldier. Learn from this his tactics: the archer does not dare to draw near; he shoots his darts from afar.

What, then? Has God only made ready the armor? No! He has also prepared a food which is more powerful than any armor, so that you may not weary in the fight, and that you may dine joyously and then win the advantage over the wicked one. If the devil merely sees you returning from the Master's banquet, he flees faster than any wind, as if he had seen a lion breathing forth flames from his mouth. If you show him a tongue stained with the precious blood, he will not be able to make a stand; if you show him your mouth all crimsoned and ruddy, cowardly beast that he is, he will run away.

ST. JOHN CHRYSOSTOM [57]

A young man must be a hero today to resist the temptations that surround him, to be the lonely believer in a despised doctrine, to face the arguments, the blasphemy, the scurrility which fill our books, our newspapers, and our streets, without giving way a finger's breadth—to resist his family and his friends, to be one against many, to be faithful against all. Nevertheless, be of good heart. Remember: *I have conquered the world.* [Jn. 16, 33] Don't dream that your sacrifice will diminish you. On the contrary, you will be quite marvelously augmented. It is by and through *virtue* that a man is manly. Chastity will render you vigorous, prompt, alert, acute—clear as a bugle call and resplendent as the sun at its rising. Life will seem to you full of savour and significance, a world of reason as well as of beauty. The further you advance, the more easy will everything become. You will laugh at the obstacles which frown on you now. As for all these poets and writers, these great names that have overshadowed your youth, suddenly the flimsiness and grotesque of all of them will reach you. You will perceive—I do not say the poverty—but the sheer nothingness of the anti-Christian ideology. For there is

81

no science save in unity, there is no dialectic save by the Yes and the No, and he who withdraws the Word destroys speech. . . .

One sentence in your letter made me laugh. It was when you told me you feared that in religion you might find an end to your quest—an end to strife. Dear friend, the day you receive God, you will have a guest within you who will never leave you repose. *I have not come to bring peace, but a sword.* [Mt. 10, 34] On that day you will know the ferment no earthly vessel can contain, the true strife against passion and spiritual darkness, the real battle—not that in which a man falls, but that from which he emerges victor.

PAUL CLAUDEL [58]

Forgive your brother from your heart. (Gospel)

The old commandment, fifth of the Ten from Sinai, runs: *Thou shalt not kill.* Jesus seizes upon the wickedness that is expressed by murder and traces it back to its origin in the murderer's heart. What breaks out in violence is already present in the evil word or intent, or rather, everything that follows is the result of that intent. The intent then, not the deed that expresses it, is decisive. Notice that Jesus does not even mention downright hatred; a brother's irritation or having "anything against thee" is enough to sow the dragon-seed of evil. From irritation grows anger; from anger the word; from the word the deed. . . .

The Old Law used justice as its norm of human behavior. As others treat you, so shall you treat them. Violence may be returned for violence, evil for evil. The justice of the day consisted in not returning more evil than the amount received, and naturally one was allowed to protect oneself from anything that seemed threatening. Christ says: That is not enough. As long as you cling to "justice" you will never be guiltless of injustice. As long as you are entangled in wrong and revenge, blow and counterblow, aggression and defense, you will be constantly drawn into fresh wrong. Passion, by its very definition, surpasses measure—quite aside from the fact that the claim to vengeance in itself is wrong because it lies outside our given role of creature. He who takes it upon himself to avenge trampled justice never

82

restores justice. The moment discussion of wrong begins, wrong stirs in one's own heart, and the result is new injustice.

If you really want to get anywhere, you must extricate yourself from the whole embroilment and seek a position far removed from all pro's and con's. You must introduce a new force, not that of self-assertion, but of selflessness; not so-called justice, but creative freedom. Man is really just only when he seeks more than mere justice. More not merely quantitatively, but qualitatively. He must find a power capable of breaking the ban of injustice, something strong enough and big enough to intercept aggression and disarm it: love.

ROMANO GUARDINI [59]

TWENTY-SECOND SUNDAY AFTER PENTECOST

The Nature of Christian Citizenship.

Then Celsus next exhorts us to help the emperor with all our power, and cooperate with him in what is right, and fight for him, and be fellow-soldiers if he presses for this, and fellow-generals with him. We may reply to this that at appropriate times we render to the emperors divine help, if I may so say, by taking up even the whole armour of God. And this we do in obedience to the apostolic utterance which says: *I exhort you, therefore, first to make prayers, supplications, intercessions, and thanksgivings for all men, for emperors, and all that are in authority.* [1 Tim. 2, 1–2] Indeed, the more pious a man is, the more effective he is in helping the emperors—more so than the soldiers who go out into the lines and kill all the enemy troops that they can.

We would also say this to those who are alien to our faith and ask us to fight for the community and to kill men: that it is also your opinion that the priests of certain images and wardens of the temples of the gods, as you think them to be, should keep their right hand undefiled for the sake of the sacrifices, that they may offer the customary sacrifices to those who you say are gods with hands unstained by blood and pure from murders. And in fact when war comes you do not enlist the priests. If, then, this is reasonable, how much more reasonable is it that, while others fight, Christians also should be fighting as priests and worshippers of God, keeping their right hands pure and by their prayers to God striving for those who fight in a righteous cause and for the emperor who reigns righteously, in order that everything which is opposed and hostile to those who act rightly may be destroyed? Moreover, we who by our prayers destroy all daemons which stir up wars, violate oaths, and disturb the peace, are of more help to the emperors than those who seem to be doing the fighting. We who offer prayers with righteousness, together with ascetic practices and exercises which teach us to despise pleasures and not to be led by them, are cooperating in the tasks of the community. Even more do we fight on behalf of the emperor. And though we do not become fellow-soldiers with him, even if he presses for this, yet we are fighting for him and composing a special army of piety through our intercessions to God.

ORIGEN [60]

Thomas More argues the rights of conscience against a tyrannical government.

Now have I heard since that some say that this obstinate manner of mine, in still refusing the oath, shall peradventure force and drive the king's Grace to make further law for me. I cannot let such a law to be made. But I am very sure that if I died by such a law I should die for that point innocent afore God. . . . Albeit, mine own good daughter, that I found myself (I cry God mercy) very sensual and my flesh much more shrinking from pain and from death than me thought it the part of a faithful Christian man, in such a case as my conscience gave me that in the saving of my body should stand the loss of my soul, yet I thank our Lord that in that conflict the spirit had in conclusion the mastery; and reason with help of faith finally concluded that for to be put to death wrongfully for doing well (as I am very sure I do in refusing to swear against mine own conscience, being such as I am not upon peril of my soul bound to change, whether my death should come without law or by colour of law), it is a case in

which a man may lose his head yet have no harm, but instead of
harm inestimable good at the hand of God.

ST. THOMAS MORE [61]

TWENTY-THIRD SUNDAY AFTER PENTECOST

We await the Saviour. (Epistle)

Now the first great and obvious characteristic of a Bible Christian, if I may use that much abused term, is to be without worldly
ties or objects, to be living in this world, but not for this world.
St. Paul says, *our conversation is in heaven* [Phil. 3, 20], or in
other words, heaven is our city. We know what it is to be a citizen of this world; it is to have interests, rights, privileges, duties,
connexions, in some particular town or state; to depend upon it,
and to be bound to defend it; to be part of it. Now all this the
Christian is in respect to heaven. Heaven is his city, earth is not.
Or, at least, so it was as regards the Christians of Scripture. *Here,*
as the same Apostle says in another place, *we have no continuing
city, but we seek one to come.* [Heb. 13, 14] And therefore he
adds to the former of these texts, *from whence also we look for
the Saviour, the Lord Jesus Christ.* This is the very definition of a
Christian, —one who looks for Christ; not who looks for gain, or
distinction, or power, or pleasure, or comfort, but who looks *for
the Saviour, the Lord Jesus Christ.* This, according to Scripture,
is the essential mark, this is the foundation of a Christian, from
which every thing else follows; whether he is rich or poor, high or
low, is a further matter, which may be considered apart; but he
surely is a primitive Christian, and he only, who has no aim of
this world, who has no wish to be other in this world than he is;
whose thoughts and aims have relation to the unseen, the future
world; who has lost his taste for this world, sweet and bitter being
the same to him; who fulfills the same Apostle's exhortation in
another Epistle, *Set your affection on things above, not on things
on the earth, for you are dead, and your life is hid with Christ in*

85

*God. When Christ, who is our life, shall appear, then shall you
also appear with Him in glory.* [Col. 3, 2–4]

JOHN HENRY NEWMAN [62]

The Savior . . . who will refashion our lowly bodies. (Epistle)
Jesus restores man to his primeval state.

God made man without evil, upright, virtuous, free from pain
and care, glorified with every virtue, adorned with all that is
good, a second microcosm within the great world, another angel
capable of worship, compounded of many things, surveying the
visible creation and initiated into the mysteries of the realm of the
mind, king over the things of the earth but subject to a higher
King of the earth and of heaven, temporal and eternal, belonging
to the realm of sight and the realm of mind, midway between
greatness and lowliness, spirit and flesh: for he is spirit by grace
and flesh by overweening pride: spirit that he may abide and
glorify his benefactor, and flesh that he may suffer, and suffering
may be admonished and disciplined when he prides himself on his
greatness. Here in this present life his life is ordered like an ani-
mal's, but elsewhere in the ages to come he is changed and—to
complete the mystery—he becomes deified by merely inclining
himself towards God; and he becomes deified in sharing in the
divine glory rather than being changed into a divine being.

ST. JOHN OF DAMASCUS [63]

*They have toiled with me in the gospel . . . my fellow workers
whose names are in the book of life.* (Epistle)

What specifically characterizes the laity is their secular nature. It
is true that those in holy orders can at times be engaged in secular
activities, and even have a secular profession. But they are, by
reason of their particular vocation, especially and professedly ordained to the sacred ministry. Similarly, by their state in life,
religious give splendid and striking testimony that the world cannot be transformed and offered to God without the spirit of the
beatitudes. But the laity, by their special vocation, seek the king-

dom of God by engaging in temporal affairs and by ordering them according to the plan of God. They live in the world, that is, in each and in all of the secular professions and occupations. They live in the ordinary circumstances of family and social life, from which the very web of their existence is woven. Today they are called by God that by exercising their proper function, and led by the spirit of the Gospel, they may work for the sanctification of the world from within as a leaven. In this way they make Christ known to others, especially by the testimony of a life resplendent in faith, hope, and charity. Therefore, since they are tightly bound up in all types of temporal affairs, it is their special task to order and to throw light upon these affairs in such a way that they may be made and grow according to Christ to the praise of the creator and redeemer.

CONSTITUTION ON THE CHURCH [64]

LAST SUNDAY AFTER PENTECOST

The sign of the Son of Man will appear in heaven. (Gospel)

The words of our Saviour are thought very hard and grievous when He says: *Forsake yourselves, take the Cross and follow Me.* [Mk. 8, 34] But it shall be much more grievous to hear these words at the Last Judgment: *Go from Me, you cursed, into the fire that shall last forever.* [Mt. 25, 41] But those who now gladly hear and follow the words of Christ, by which He counsels them to follow Him, shall not then need to fear, hearing those words of everlasting damnation. The sign of the Cross shall appear in heaven when our Lord shall come to judge the world, and the servants of the Cross, who conformed themselves here in this life to Christ crucified on the Cross, shall go to Christ their judge with great faith and trust.

Why, then, do you dread to take His Cross, since it is the very way to the kingdom of heaven, and there is no other way? In the Cross is health, in the Cross is life; in the Cross is the fullness of heavenly sweetness; in the Cross is strength of mind, joy of spirit, height of virtue, full perfection of all holiness, and there is no help for the soul, or hope of everlasting life, save through the virtue of the Cross.

Take, therefore, your cross and follow Jesus, and you shall go to life everlasting. He has gone before you, bearing His Cross, and died for you upon that Cross so that you should in like manner bear with Him the cross of penance and tribulation, and that you should be ready in like manner for His love to suffer death, if need be, as He has done for you. If you die with Him you will live with Him; if you are His companion with Him in pain, you will be His companion in glory.

Behold, then, how on the Cross all things stand; and how, in dying to the world, lies all our health; and that there is no other way to life and true inward peace but the way of the Cross, and the way of daily submission of the body to the spirit. Go wherever you will, and reap whatever you desire, and you will never find, above you or beneath you, within you or without you, a more high, a more excellent, a more sure way to Christ than the way of the Holy Cross.

Arrange everything after your own will, and yet you will find that you must of necessity suffer something, either according to your will or against it, and so you will always find the Cross. You will either feel pain in your body or have trouble of spirit in your soul. You will be sometimes as if you were forsaken by God; sometimes you will be vexed with your neighbor and, what is yet more painful, you will sometimes be a burden to yourself. And you will find no means of deliverance save that it behooves you to suffer until it please Almighty God of His goodness to dispose otherwise for you. He desires that you should learn to suffer tribulation without consolation, so that you may learn to submit yourself wholly to Him, and by tribulation to be made more humble than you were at first. No man feels the Passion of Christ so efficaciously as he who feels pain like the pain Christ felt.

This Cross is always ready, and everywhere it awaits you, and you cannot flee it nor fully escape it, wherever you go. For, wherever you go, you will always bear yourself about with you, and so you will always find yourself. Turn where you will, above yourself and beneath yourself, within and without yourself, and you will find this Cross on every side, so that it will be necessary for you to keep yourself always in patience, and it behooves you to do this if you will have inward peace and deserve a perpetual crown in heaven.

THOMAS A KEMPIS [65]

Christianity is a growing, a becoming. Christianity is a sowing, is a Messianic time of transition. It is a growing, a becoming, because Christ, too, is this in his fulfilment as the Mystical Christ. Christianity is the unfolding in space and time of the humanity of Christ. For ever, at all times, in all places the Incarnate Son, the Head of the Body, joins new members to himself, till his consummation, his fulness, his $\pi\lambda\dot{\eta}\rho\omega\mu\varkappa$ is reached. [Eph. 1, 23] To the end he bears in his members the form of a servant. Only when by the Will of the Father this world-era, this Messianic interval, is closed, when the day of the harvest, the new world-period dawns, everlasting and imperishable, only then will there be an end of this eschatological and Christological tension. In the place of the Messianic, the Christian era, there will arise that of the Trinity, the era of the Triune God. As Head of the Body Christ will give back his Messianic power into the Father's hands. *When all things shall be subdued unto him, then the Son also shall be subject unto him that put all things under him, that God may be all in all.* [1 Cor. 15, 28] Christianity is essentially an eschatology, a pressing forward towards future perfection.

KARL ADAM [66]

The Coming of Christ will have for its purpose certain divine works, no less mighty than those which have already been performed, but more glorious. These works take their place in the sequence of God's works at the various stages of sacred history. This Coming is their supreme expression. The first of these works is Judgement. Judgement is the work by which Righteousness, which is God's faithfulness to Himself, performs its work. This Rigthteousness is entirely positive; it is the fulfilment of the promises made by God. And Judgement is that fulfilment. It is manifestation; in other words, it brings to an end the order of present things, in which true values are hidden and false values are apparent. Judgement exposes the nothingness of that which is not founded upon God, and it necessarily condemns that which is not founded upon God. And it reveals, on the other hand, that what is truly founded upon God has been established forever. It is the manifestation of the truth. And it manifests the fact that the truth is Christ. It bears witness, then, that those who have believed in Christ have lived in the truth. Thus *it will be for him to prove the world wrong, about sin, and about rightness of heart; I am going back to my Father. . . . About judging; he who rules in this world has had sentence passed on him already*. [Jn. 16, 8–11]

The second divine work is Gathering. *The Son of Man . . . will send out his angels with a loud blast of the trumpet, to gather his elect from the four winds, from one end of heaven to the other*. [Mt. 24, 30–31] This Gathering was, in the Old Testament, one of the essential promises made by God through the Prophets to the scattered people. Christ had already gathered together in Himself not only the scattered people, but the divisions of mankind, and had made of them a single Church. The ancient Liturgy described the day of the final Gathering of those who were thus united but remained separate: "Gather, O Lord, thy Church, from the towns and cities and markets, from the four corners of the universe" [*Didache* 10, 3]. This is to be the fulfilment of the priestly prayer *that they should all be one, as we are one*. [Jn. 17, 22] For unity is a divine work. It is the mark of the life of the Trinity. And the unity of the Church is her visible Epiphany.

Finally there is Resurrection, the repercussion through bodies and the whole cosmos of that which was already accomplished in the Person of Christ. Resurrection is not merely the bringing back to life of bodies for the purpose of judgement, the general resurrection of the just and the unjust. It is the divine act that bestows incorruptibility upon the bodies of the saints and delivers them from the slavery of spiritual death. Thus the action of God reaches out to the utmost bounds of His creation. For God the Redeemer is also God the Creator. He wishes to lose nothing of the creation that is His. Thus, too, the cosmic meaning of the Parousia is revealed in its entirety. Beyond humanity it reaches out to the whole cosmos and raises up the new heaven and the new earth.

JEAN DANIELOU [67]

Sanctoral

DRYNESS

That man is perfect in faith who can come to God in the utter dearth of his feelings and desires, without a glow or an aspiration, with the weight of low thoughts, failures, neglects, and wandering forgetfulness, and say to him, "Thou art my refuge."

GEORGE MACDONALD [68]

June

St. John the Baptist
Sts. Peter and Paul
Commemoration of St. Paul

ST. JOHN THE BAPTIST

Since in the fourth century December 25 was adopted for the nativity of Christ, it was natural that the birthday of his Forerunner should be celebrated six months earlier, according to the indications of St. Luke. [1, 36] The choice of the summer and winter solstices for these two nativity feasts coincided nicely with John's remark: "He must increase, I must decrease." [Jn. 3, 30]

There was a man sent from God whose name was John. (Gospel)

Whom, my brethren, can we conceive to have such majestic and severe sanctity as the Holy Baptist? He had a privilege which reached near upon the prerogative of the Most Blessed Mother of God; for, if she was conceived without sin, at least without sin he was born. She was all-pure, all-holy, and sin had no part in her: but St. John was in the beginning of his existence a partaker of Adam's curse: he lay under God's wrath, deprived of that grace which Adam had received, and which is the life and strength of human nature. Yet as soon as Christ, his Lord and Saviour, came to him, and Mary saluted his own mother, Elizabeth, forthwith the grace of God was given to him, and the original guilt was wiped away from his soul. And therefore it is that we celebrate the nativity of St. John; nothing unholy does the Church celebrate; not St. Peter's nor St. Paul's, nor St. Augustine's, nor St. Gregory's, nor St. Bernard's, nor St. Aloysius's, nor the nativity of any other Saint, however glorious, because they were all born in sin. She celebrates their conversions, their prerogatives, their martyrdoms, their deaths, their translations, but not their birth, because in no case was it holy. Three nativities alone does she commemorate, our Lord's, His Mother's, and lastly, St. John's. What a special gift was this, my brethren, separating the Baptist off, and distinguishing him from all prophets and preachers, who ever lived, however holy, except perhaps the prophet Jeremias! And such as was his commencement, was the course of his life. He was carried away by the Spirit into the desert, and there he lived on the simplest fare, in the rudest clothing, in the caves of wild beasts, apart from men, for thirty years, leading a life of mortification and of meditation, till he was called to preach penance, to proclaim the Christ, and to baptize Him; and then having done his work, and having left no act of sin on record, he was laid aside as an instrument which had lost its use, and languished in prison, till he was suddenly cut off by the sword of the executioner. Sanctity is the one idea of him impressed upon us from first to last; a most marvellous Saint, a hermit from his childhood, then a preacher to a fallen people, and then a Martyr. Surely such a life fulfills the expectation, which the salutation of Mary raised concerning him before his birth.

JOHN HENRY NEWMAN [69]

Baptism is the ending of the old covenant and the beginning of the new. For the inauguration of the new was John, than whom there was none greater *among them that are born of women,* the crown indeed of the prophets. *For all the prophets and the law prophesied until John.* [Mt. 11, 11–13] But of the Gospel dispensation he was the first-fruits, for (we read) *the beginning of the gospel of Jesus Christ* and after some words *John did baptize in the wilderness.* [Mk. 1, 1.4] I grant you that Elijah the Tishbite was taken up to heaven: yet he was not greater than John. Enoch was translated but was not greater than John. Moses was the greatest of lawgivers and all the prophets were admirable, but they were not greater than John. I dare not compare prophet with prophet, but it was their Master and ours that declared *among those that are born of women, there hath not risen a greater than John.* [Mt. 11, 11] Not "born of virgins" observe! but "born of women." We are comparing a head-servant with his fellow-servants, not the Son with the household, for his pre-eminence and grace are incomparable. Of this grace, do you observe what manner of man God chose to be the inaugurator? One who forsook possessions and loved solitude, but no misanthrope. He fed on locusts to make his soul grow wings. Sated with honey, the words he spoke were sweeter than honey and of more profit. Clothed in a garment of camel's hair, he exemplified in his own person the ascetic life. While he was yet cradled in his mother's womb, he was hallowed by the Holy Spirit. Jeremiah also was

95

sanctified before he came forth out of his mother's womb, but did not then prophesy. Only John *leaped in his mother's womb for joy* [Lk. 1, 44] and in the Spirit recognized his Master, when his fleshly eyes were blind. For since the grace of baptism was so great, its minister too must needs be great.

ST. CYRIL OF JERUSALEM [70]

JUNE 29
STS. PETER AND PAUL

Peter "presiding in love" in his successors.

Although, dearly beloved, we be found both weak and slothful in fulfilling the duties of our office, because, whatever devoted and vigorous action we desire to do, we are hindered by the frailty of our very condition; yet having the unceasing propitiation of the Almighty and perpetual Priest, who being like us and yet equal with the Father, brought down His Godhead even to things human, and raised His Manhood even to things Divine, we worthily and piously rejoice over His dispensation, whereby, though He has delegated the care of His sheep to many shepherds, yet He has not Himself abandoned the guardianship of His beloved flock, and from His overruling and eternal protection we have received the support of the Apostles' aid also, which assuredly does not cease from its operation: and the strength of the foundation, on which the whole superstructure of the Church is reared, is not weakened by the weight of the temple that rests upon it. For the solidity of that faith which was praised in the chief of the Apostles is perpetual: and as that remains which Peter believed in Christ, so that remains which Christ instituted in Peter. For when, as has been read in the Gospel lesson, the Lord had asked the disciples whom they believed Him to be amid the various opinions that were held, and the blessed Peter had replied, saying, *You are Christ, the Son of the living God* [Mt. 16, 16], the Lord says, *Blessed are you, Simon Bar-Jona, because flesh and blood*

*has not revealed it to you, but my Father, who is in heaven.
And I say to you, that you are Peter and upon this rock will I
build My Church, and the gates of Hades shall not prevail against
it. And I will give to you the keys of the kingdom of heaven. And
whatsoever you shall bind on earth, shall be bound in heaven;
and whatsoever you shall loose on earth, shall be loosed also in
heaven.* [16, 17-19]

The dispensation of Truth therefore abides, and the blessed
Peter persevering in the strength of the Rock, which he has received, has not abandoned the helm of the Church, which he
undertook. For he was ordained before the rest in such a way
that from his being called the Rock, from his being pronounced
the Foundation, from his being constituted the Doorkeeper of the
kingdom of heaven, from his being set as the Umpire to bind and
to loose, whose judgments shall retain their validity in heaven,
from all these mystical titles we might know the nature of his
association with Christ. And still to-day he more fully and effec-
tually performs what is entrusted to him, and carries out every
part of his duty and charge in Him and with Him, through
Whom he has been glorified. And so if anything is won from the
mercy of God by our daily supplications, it is of his work and
merits whose power lives and whose authority prevails in his See.
For this, dearly beloved, was gained by that confession, which,
inspired in the Apostle's heart by God the Father, transcended all
the uncertainty of human opinions, and was endued with the
firmness of a rock, which no assaults could shake. For throughout the Church Peter daily says, *You are Christ, the Son of the
living God,* and every tongue which confesses the Lord, accepts
the instruction his voice conveys. This Faith conquers the devil,
and breaks the bonds of his prisoners. It uproots us from this
earth and plants us in heaven, and the gates of Hades cannot
prevail against it. For with such solidity is it endued by God that
the depravity of heretics cannot mar it nor the unbelief of the
heathen overcome it.

ST. LEO THE GREAT [71]

Rome, the first in the Church episcopally—decidedly so and
from the start—is still present, more alive than ever. Why and by

97

what right should one look elsewhere for this needed "universal rector" when he is here, appealing now these two thousand years only to Saint Peter? Saint Peter, inferior in gifts, in personal activity, in evangelical success to his youngest brother Saint Paul. Saint Peter, equal in his apostolic calling and in his share of the missionary charism with his companions and compartners, the "Twelve." Yet Saint Peter, chosen as the leader of the apostles of Christ, always first in the gospel lists, asked to *strengthen his brothers* [Lk. 22, 32] and (from Pentecost on) taking the initiative, the collegial command—collegial but command all the same —of the whole Christian dynamism and structure. Saint Peter, consequently, superior in this to the other apostles; *primus inter pares,* "first amongst equals." Yes, the apostles are his—Peter's— equals, except obviously for his quality of "first." This quality does not take him out of his human condition nor out of the rank of apostle, but gives him the responsibilities and, consequently, the prerogatives of "universal rector." These prerogatives must harmonize with the collegiality of the apostolic group that the primacy should serve. And that is why the primacy cannot be dependent on it and yet it imposes on the "Primate" the obligation of respecting the group's mission and each of its members. This group of which he is and remains part, for whose authority his own authority over it has been given him: this group is with him the visible continuation in the world of the Word's activity, the Word come forth from God and become the "savior." The "cornerstone" of the Christian abode, in perpetual living construction, is Christ alone. Yet the edifice of salvation is being built every day on the foundation of the twelve living pillars, mentioned in the Apocalypse (21, 14). And these are the apostles, the episcopate. But did not the Builder himself call one amongst them the "rock" in a very special manner?

ORESTE KERAME [72]

JUNE 30

COMMEMORATION OF ST. PAUL

In order to provide better possibilities for the full liturgical celebration of the memory of the two great apostles, June 30 is set aside in a special way to commemorate the apostle to the Gentiles.

On the road to Ostia, about five hundred yards from the gate of the city, was a private cemetery belonging to a Christian family; Paul's friends and disciples transported his mortal remains there. A monument was erected there which was judiciously given the form of a victory trophy; the priest Gaius, at the beginning of the third century, gave a description of it. A simple epitaph was engraved on it: *Paul, Apostle, martyr.* This sufficed; therein all was said.

Paul, Apostle, martyr . . . Yes, this tells the tale. In these three words is assumed and summed up the prodigious destiny of the little Jew of Tarsus, whom the personal will of God made the most extraordinary of all His witnesses. Since that splendid hour at the height of noon, when, on the sandy trail, Jesus appeared before the prostrate Saul, until this gray morning, when on the road to Ostia, his blood was poured out as a libation, not a day had passed which he had not given to the cause of Christ; not a single thought or effort which had not tended to establish His glory. Martyrdom was the normal conclusion of this destiny, for it would have been inadmissible that he should not consummate his total sacrifice—he who had wished to complete in his flesh what was lacking in the sufferings of Christ and to be nailed to the Cross with Him. But there was to be an immense number of martyrs in the Church's history; their blood was to be, according to the famous expression of Tertullian, "the seed of Christians"; among them Paul occupies a unique, exceptional place, which the Church has always acknowledged.

An apostle, yes. He was an apostle, as he said himself, and as all Christian tradition has proclaimed. As much as those dozen Galilean fishermen and farmers whom Jesus had appointed to follow Him, the Rabbi Saul had a right to this title and he laid claim to it legitimately. It is indeed false to pretend, as some do, that he was the inventor of Christianity and that the teaching of Jesus would not exist without him; for the Gospel which he preached was substantially the same as that of the other Apostles and he did no more than define, clarify, and distribute the treasures which the Master Himself had given. But it is beyond doubt

99

that, without him, Christianity would not be exactly as we know it. It has been said of him that he was "the first after the Unique"; his role was such that we cannot understand Jesus and His Word without referring to the saintly genius of Tarsus—to his message and to his deeds.

It is in his letters that we must find and hear Paul's message—in those imperishable letters which we have merely touched on. . . . It is to these we must resort, and the revelations enclosed there will emerge with their great shattering bursts of light. Is it not true that at Mass, when the reading of the Epistle brings us some brief passage, our impression is one of an immediate shock, which reaches the depth of our souls and suddenly illuminates the anguished darkness of the world and of ourselves?

The centuries flow by and events move on, but the message of Saint Paul remains; nothing shall ever invalidate it. For anyone who considers his example, for anyone who hears his words, there emerge lessons which are ever new.

To the helpless feeling of negation and absurdity which is, for all of us, the worst temptation of the conscience, Paul opposes the unshakable certainty that there is a supernatural explanation, an ultimate revelation, which definitively sets forth the meaning of life.

In the face of the great treason of man, that universal oblivion into which the world is plunging, he declares, with unique persuasive power, the reality of a presence which no philosophy can abolish and whose infinite mercy no treason can discourage.

Before that feeling of despair which man draws from the very heart of his condition, and which penetrates the inmost fibers of an era like ours, what he says, repeats, and proclaims is that there is no ineluctable fatality, that redeemed man has a promise of glory: "O death, where is thy victory? O death, where is thy sting?" [1 Cor. 15, 55]

And in a universe of hatred and violence, the positive contribution of the great Apostle is something he has received from Christ Himself and has expressed in deathless words; the message of Charity, the omnipotence of Love.

For us Christians, Saint Paul is unquestionably the most wonderful example of that pure and ardent flame which Christ Jesus can light in the souls of those who love Him. And even for those who do not share his faith, he remains a genius, a hero, the champion of causes which are more precious than life itself, a man who is a credit to mankind.

HENRI DANIEL-ROPS [73]

July

The Precious Blood
The Visitation
St. Irenaeus
Sts. Cyril and Methodius
St. Thomas More
St. Mary Magdalen
St. Ignatius of Loyola

JULY 1

FEAST OF THE PRECIOUS BLOOD

This is a recent feast of the Roman Liturgy instituted by Pope Pius IX in 1848 and raised to the rank of a first-class feast in 1934 by Pope Pius XI to commemorate the nineteenth centenary of our redemption.

By means of this feast and others (for example, Holy Cross, Sacred Heart, Sorrows of Mary), the Church keeps alive the memory of the love and passion of Christ throughout the whole year.

The terrible seriousness of his love.

It was there, there on that slab of stone, . . . that the bloodless body of Jesus lay during the first Holy Saturday. There had been blood everywhere. All the blood that that body had contained had been drawn through the stripes with which it had been lacerated, through the wounds in the hands, in the feet, on the head, in the side, and the last of it had run down the Cross into the arid earth of Calvary, twenty yards away from here. There had been blood on the tiled floor of the praetorium, blood on the column of the flagellation, blood on the soldier's whips, blood on the scarlet cloak. There had been blood on the stones of the city streets, in the dust of the road leading to Golgotha, on Veronica's veil. Jesus had left his blood everywhere he had passed on this soil of Palestine, his own country, in this city of Jerusalem that he had so greatly loved.

None of all that had happened was the result of accident, none of it was just a symbol; it was an utterly terrible human reality. And now the scars left by the wounds on the hands and the feet and the side have made their lasting imprint upon a human body united for ever to the divinity in the Person of the Word. They bear an eternal witness to this blood which, on a certain day in the history of mankind, was shed for us here on our earth.

There had indeed been nothing accidental about it all. Jesus had to die thus, because it had been God's idea—his very certain,

103

very precise and detailed idea—since the beginnings of humanity, like the ambitions for the future that a father and mother cherish in their hearts as they watch a son grow up. Jesus had to give his Father, and also his brothers, us men, the proof of his love and his obedience by shedding all his blood in suffering. . . .

Jesus came to us thus by a path of blood and sweat, so as to prove to us both the terrible seriousness of his love and his will to redeem us. But was it not also the purpose of this descent of love in the rent and tortured flesh to convince us that this work of purification, of re-creation, goes to the most obscure depths of our human nature, to where our sins, our denials, our weaknesses and our sicknesses of the body and of the soul take root? When things go badly, when we are, as it were, physically weighed down by sin, by temptation, or simply by the load of our incapacities and frustrations, we need to be able to remind ourselves that the blood of our beloved Saviour and Doctor is there within our reach. Jesus so wished that his blood should remain within our reach that he made its presence among us permanent under the species of the wine in the mystery of the Eucharistic sacrifice.

RENE VOILLAUME [74]

The power of his blood.

That which really gives life, often gives, through the defects of those who receive it, death; that is to say, the precious Blood of My only-begotten Son, which destroyed death and darkness, and gave life and truth, and confounded falsehood. For I give this Blood and use It for salvation and perfection in the case of that man who disposes himself properly to receive it, for It gives life and adorns the soul with every grace, in proportion to the disposition and affection of him who receives It; similarly It gives death to him who receives It unworthily, living in iniquity and in the darkness of mortal sin; to him, I say, It gives death and not life; not through defect of the Blood, nor through defect of the minister, though there might be great evil in him, because its evil would not spoil nor defile the Blood nor diminish Its grace and virtue, nor does an evil minister do harm to him to whom he gives the Blood, but to himself he does the harm of guilt, which will be followed by punishment, unless he correct himself with contrition and repentance. I say then that the Blood does harm to him who receives it unworthily, not through defect of the Blood, nor of the minister, but through his own evil disposition and defect inasmuch as he has befouled his mind and body with such impurity and misery, and has been so cruel to himself and his neighbour. He has used cruelty to himself, depriving himself of grace, trampling under the feet of his affection the fruit of the Blood which he had received in Holy Baptism, when the stain of original sin was taken from him by virtue of the Blood.

ST. CATHERINE OF SIENA [75]

JULY 2

THE VISITATION OF MARY TO ELIZABETH

Only a few days after the feast commemorating the miraculous birth of John the Baptist, the Church invites us to commemorate Mary's journey to Hebron and the sanctification of the Forerunner in his mother's womb. This feast was instituted in 1389 by Pope Urban VI to ask for the healing of the papal schism which was racking the Church. This explains the references to peace in the text of the Mass.

And Mary rising up in those days went into the hill country with haste, into a city of Juda. [Lk. 1, 39]

How lyrical that is, the opening sentence of St. Luke's description of the Visitation. We can feel the rush of warmth and kindness, the sudden urgency of love that sent that girl hurrying over the hills. "Those days" in which she rose on that impulse were the days in which Christ was being formed in her, the impulse was his impulse.

Many women, if they were expecting a child, would refuse to hurry over the hills on a visit of pure kindness. They would say they had a duty to themselves and to their unborn child which came before anything or anyone else.

The Mother of God considered no such thing. Elizabeth was

105

going to have a child, too, and although Mary's own child was God, she could not forget Elizabeth's need—almost incredible to us, but characteristic of her.

She greeted her cousin Elizabeth, and at the sound of her voice, John quickened in his mother's womb and leapt for joy.

I am come, said Christ, *that they may have life and may have it more abundantly.* [Jn. 10, 10] Even before He was born His presence gave life.

With what piercing shoots of joy does this story of Christ unfold! First the conception of a child in a child's heart, and then this first salutation, an infant leaping for joy in his mother's womb, knowing the hidden Christ and leaping into life.

How did Elizabeth herself know what had happened to Our Lady? What made her realize that this little cousin who was so familiar to her was the mother of her God?

She knew it by the child within herself, by the quickening into life which was a leap of joy.

If we practice this contemplation taught and shown to us by Our Lady, we will find that our experience is like hers.

If Christ is growing in us, if we are at peace, recollected, because we know that however insignificant our life seems to be, from it He is forming Himself; if we go with eager wills, "in haste," to wherever our circumstances compel us, because we believe that He desires to be in that place, we shall find that we are driven more and more to act on the impulse of His love.

And the answer we shall get from others to those impulses will be an awakening into life, or the leap into joy of the already wakened life within them.

It is not necessary at this stage of our contemplation to speak to others of the mystery of life growing in us. It is only necessary to give ourselves to that life, all that we are, to pray without ceasing, not by a continual effort to concentrate our minds but by a growing awareness that Christ is being formed in our lives from what we are. We must trust Him for this, because it is not a time to see His face, we must possess Him secretly and in darkness, as the earth possesses the seed. We must not try to force Christ's growth in us, but with a deep gratitude for the light burning secretly in our darkness, we must fold our concentrated love upon Him like earth, surrounding, holding, and nourishing the seed.

We must be swift to obey the winged impulses of His Love, carrying Him to wherever He longs to be; and those who recognize His presence will be stirred, like Elizabeth, with new life. They will know His presence, not by any special beauty or power shown by us, but in the way that the bud knows the presence of the light, by an unfolding in themselves, a putting forth of their own beauty.

It seems that this is Christ's favorite way of being recognized, that He prefers to be known, not by His own human features, but by the quickening of His own life in the heart, which is the response to His coming.

When John recognized Him, He was hidden in His mother's womb. After the Resurrection He was known, not by His familiar features, but by the love in Magdalene's heart, the fire in the hearts of the travellers to Emmaus, and the wound in his own heart handled by Thomas.

CARYLL HOUSELANDER [76]

JULY 3

ST. IRENAEUS

A disciple of Polycarp who was a disciple of John the Apostle, Irenaeus was bishop of Lyons at the end of the second century. He is both a witness to primitive tradition and one of the Church's first great theologians. His writings are particularly valuable for their defense of apostolic tradition against Gnosticism, the great ideological threat to Christian orthodoxy in the second century. He died during the persecution of the emperor, Septimius Severus in 202 A.D.

The faith of the Church.

The church, though dispersed throughout the whole world, even to the ends of the earth, has received from the apostles and their disciples this faith: She believes in one God, the Father Almighty, Maker of heaven, and earth, and the sea, and all things that are in them; and in one Christ Jesus, the Son of God, who became incarnate for our salvation; and in the Holy Spirit, who proclaimed through the prophets the dispensations of God, and the advents, and the birth from a virgin, and the passion, and the resurrection from the dead, and the ascension into heaven in the flesh of the beloved Christ Jesus, our Lord, and His future manifestation from heaven in the glory of the Father *to gather all things in one* [Eph. 1, 10], and to raise up anew all flesh of the whole human race, in order that to Christ Jesus, our Lord, and God, and Saviour, and King, according to the will of the invisible Father, *every knee should bow, of things in heaven, and things in earth, and things under the earth, and that every tongue should confess* [Phil. 2, 10] to Him, and that He should execute just judgment towards all; that He may send spiritual wickednesses, and the angels who transgressed and became apostates, together with the ungodly, and unrighteous, and wicked, and profane among men, into everlasting fire; but may, in the exercise of His grace, confer immortality on the righteous, and holy, and those who have kept His commandments, and have persevered in His love, some from the beginning of their Christian course, and others from the date of their repentance, and may surround them with everlasting glory.

As I have already observed, the church, having received this preaching and this faith, although scattered throughout the whole world, yet, as if occupying but one house, carefully preserves it. She also believes these points of doctrine just as if she had but one soul, and one and the same heart, and she proclaims them, and teaches them, and hands them down, with perfect harmony, as if she possessed only one mouth. For, although the languages of the world are dissimilar, yet the import of the tradition is one and the same. For the churches which have been planted in Germany do not believe or hand down anything different, nor do those in Spain, nor those in Gaul, nor those in the East, nor those in Egypt, nor those in Libya, nor those which have been established in the central regions of the world. But as the sun, that creature of God, is one and the same throughout the whole world, so also the preaching of the truth shines everywhere, and enlightens all men that are willing to come to a knowledge of the truth. Nor will any one of the rulers in the churches, however highly gifted he may be in point of eloquence, teach doctrines different from these for no one is greater than the Master: nor, on the other hand, will he who is deficient in power of expression inflict injury on the tradition. For the faith being ever one and the same, neither does one who is able at great length to discourse regarding it, make any addition to it, nor does one, who can say but little, diminish it.

ST. IRENAEUS [77]

Freed from condemnation.

Man was created by God so that he might have life. If now, having lost life, wounded by the serpent, he could not return to life, but was to be finally abandoned to death, then God would be conquered and the malice of the serpent would have overcome His will. But since God is at once invincible and magnanimous, He has shown His magnanimity in correcting man and in putting all men to the test, as we have said. Yet, by the second Adam, He has bound the strong man and destroyed his arms, and He had done away with death, bringing life to man who had been subject to death. For Adam had become the possession of the devil and the devil held him in his power, having perversely deceived him in subjecting him to death when he had offered him immortality. Indeed, in promising them that they would be like gods, which was not in his power, he brought about death in them. This is why he who made man captive was himself made captive by God, and man whom he had captured found himself freed from the slavery of condemnation.

ST. IRENAEUS [78]

JULY 7
STS. CYRIL AND METHODIUS

Brothers in the apostolate as well as brothers in the flesh, Cyril and Methodius were missionaries sent out in the mid-ninth cen-

tury, by the Patriarch of Constantinople to evangelize the Kha-
zars, Bulgarians, Moravians, and Bohemians. Welcomed by the
popes, they nevertheless had much to suffer from false brethren
of the Western Church who schemed to defeat their successful
apostolate among the Slavs. Their great work of inventing a
Slavic alphabet and of translating the Bible and the liturgy into
Slavonic was particularly resented and opposed. Pope Adrian II,
however, approved their liturgical methods in 869 and conse-
crated Methodius archbishop of Pannonia. In later years (880),
after further controversy, Pope John VIII formally approved the
liturgical use of Slavonic in the following words:

"There is nothing contrary to the faith or to sound doctrine in
singing Mass or in reading the holy Gospel and the sacred lessons
from the Old and New Testaments, properly translated and ex-
pressed, or in chanting the other services in the Slavonic lan-
guage."

I am sending you out like sheep among wolves. (Gospel)

One thing was clear. This was the Negro's day. We were, at long
last, at his side. But even the newsmen were not sure why we
were there. They were not even convinced that we knew why; one
of them asked us, in words that were not especially flattering:
why have the Catholics gotten into the act? We were not sure
either, in a way that could easily be formulated. But it was something like an ethic of the guts; some things cannot be disposed of,
in peace, by moral tics over headlines, even in 1965.

Almost everyone one could think of was there: men of concern,
men of theology, nurses, teaching nuns, writers, rabbis, artists,
students. Where's so and so? He was either there (one would
meet him or see him in the crowd) or he was on his way or he
had stopped and gone. And all week long, the vigils, the prayers,
the Negro hospitality (our money was no good, anywhere), the
cheerful enduring faith, the contrast of ascetic purity and puritan-
ism on the rampage, of birth pangs and the desperate lunges of
moral death, the swift free calls to prayer and song and march,
and the knowledge that slavery hemmed us in—what is the

Church, anyway? is it where we came from, or is it here, being created by Negroes and their white acolytes?

In any case, it was the black man's day, his week; one might say, his week of creation. He had been conceived and born at Bloody Bridge, at all the bloody crossroads of the nation, weeks and years before Selma. Could he, this week, bring us over that Bridge, to birth? He might; love is a marvelous midwife.

DANIEL BERRIGAN [79]

The mission witness.

The visible Church, firmly established among a people, is the sacramental or mystical Christ doing among this people what historically He has already *done once for all who await Him.* [Heb. 9, 26]. This unique saving event happened among one particular people at one precise place and time in mankind's history. But this event is "for all." Therefore, the historical work of the redeeming Christ is sacramentally extended, in other times and places, to more and more particular peoples, through the visible Church firmly established among them, thus gradually bringing to sacramentally signified completion, in the sight and in the hearing of all men, the one salutary work already accomplished historically by Christ for all mankind. It is through the efforts and the witness of missionaries, establishing the Church among the nations who have not yet known Christ, that the one messianic mission is being progressively achieved, that the history of man's salvation is being fulfilled and the way prepared for the coming of the Lord.

EUGENE HILLMAN [80]

The harvest is great indeed, but the laborers are few. (Gospel)

Within the Church we observe all sorts of groups whose members are vowed to the perfect practice of this or that particular virtue: mercy, detachment, the splendour of the liturgy, the missions, contemplation. Why should there not be men vowed to the task

111

of exemplifying, by their lives, the general sanctification of human endeavour?—men whose common religious ideal would be to give a full and conscious explanation of the divine possibilities or demands which any worldly occupation implies—men, in a word, who would devote themselves, in the fields of thought, art, industry, commerce and politics, etc., to carrying out, in the sublime spirit these demand, the basic tasks which form the very bonework of society? Around us the "natural" progress which nourishes the sanctity of each new age is all too often left to the children of the world, that is to say to agnostics or the irreligious. Unconsciously or involuntarily, no doubt, these collaborate in the Kingdom of God and in the fulfilment of the elect: their efforts, transcending or correcting their incomplete or bad intentions, are gathered in by Him "whose energy subjects all things to itself." But that is no more than a second best, a temporary phase in the organisation of human activity. Right from the hands that knead the dough, to those that consecrate it, the great and universal Host should be prepared and handled in the spirit of *adoration*.

May the time come when men, having been awakened to a sense of the close bond linking all the movements of this world in the unique event of the Incarnation, shall be unable to give themselves to a single one of their tasks without illuminating it with the clear vision that their work—however elementary it may be—is received and made use of by a Centre of the universe.

PIERRE TEILHARD DE CHARDIN [81]

JULY 9

ST. THOMAS MORE

More was one of the many-sided geniuses of the sixteenth century. A "complete man" of "singular learning and wit," he became one of the founders of Christian humanism in England. As a lawyer he rose high in the political life of Henry Tudor's England, becoming successively speaker of the House of Commons and finally, after the fall of Cardinal Wolsey, Lord Chancellor of England. As a husband, father, and friend he was of such a gentle, sweet, and happy disposition that he was the delight of those who were his associates. But nothing availed to save him from the tyrant-king who demanded a renunciation of conscience in order to salve his own. After a cruel imprisonment and a mockery of a trial, he died on the scaffold, July 6, 1535, protesting that he died "the King's good servant but God's first."

More is a man of an angel's wit and singular learning. I know not his fellow. For where is the man of that gentleness, lowliness, and affability? And, as time requireth, a man of marvellous mirth and pastimes, and sometime of as sad gravity. A man for all seasons.

ROBERT WHITTINTON [82]

More seems to be born and made for friendship, of which he is the sincerest and most persistent devotee. Neither is he afraid of that multiplicity of friends, of which Hesiod disapproves. Accessible to every tender of intimacy, he is by no means fastidious in choosing his acquaintance, while he is most accommodating in keeping it on foot, and constant in retaining it. If he has fallen in with anyone whose faults he cannot cure, he finds some opportunity of parting with him, untying the knot of intimacy without tearing it; but when he has found any sincere friends, whose characters are suited to his own, he is so delighted with their society and conversation, that he seems to find in these the chief pleasure of life, having an absolute distaste for tennis and dice and cards, and the other games with which the mass of gentlemen beguile the tediousness of Time. It should be added that, while he is somewhat neglectful of his own interest, no one takes more pains in attending to the concerns of his friends. What more need I say? If anyone requires a perfect example of true friendship, it is in More that he will best find it.

In company his extraordinary kindness and sweetness of temper are such as to cheer the dullest spirit, and alleviate the annoyance of the most trying circumstances. From boyhood he was always so pleased with a joke, that it might seem that jesting was the main object of his life; but with all that, he did not go so far as buffoonery, nor had ever any inclination to bitterness. When quite a youth, he wrote farces and acted them. If a thing was facetiously said, even though it was aimed at himself, he was charmed with it, so much did he enjoy any witticism that had a

113

flavour of subtlety or genius. This led to his amusing himself as a young man with epigrams, and taking great delight in Lucian. Indeed, it was he that suggested my writing the Moria, or Praise of Folly, which was much the same thing as setting a camel to dance.

There is nothing that occurs in human life, from which he does not seek to extract some pleasure, although the matter may be serious in itself. If he has to do with the learned and intelligent, he is delighted with their cleverness, if with unlearned or stupid people, he finds amusement in their folly. He is not offended even by professed clowns, as he adapts himself with marvellous dexterity to the tastes of all; while with ladies generally, and even with his wife, his conversation is made up of humour and playfulness. You would say it was a second Democritus, or rather that Pythagorean philosopher, who strolls in leisurely mood through the market-place, contemplating the turmoil of those who buy and sell. There is no one less guided by the opinion of the multitude, but on the other hand no one sticks more closely to common sense. . . .

He had drunk deep of Good Letters from his earliest years; and when a young man, he applied himself to the study of Greek and of philosophy, but his father was so far from encouraging him in this pursuit, that he withdrew his allowance and almost disowned him, because he thought he was deserting his hereditary study, being himself an expert professor of English Law. For remote as that profession is from true learning, those who become masters of it have the highest rank and reputation among their countrymen; and it is difficult to find any readier way to acquire fortune and honour. Indeed a considerable part of the nobility of that island has had its origin in this profession, in which it is said that no one can be perfect, unless he has toiled at it for many years. It was natural, that in his younger days our friend's genius, born for better things, should shrink from this study; nevertheless, after he had a taste of the learning of the Schools, he became so conversant with it, that there was no one more eagerly consulted by suitors; and the income that he made by it was not surpassed by any of those who did nothing else; such was the power and quickness of his intellect.

He also expended considerable labour in perusing the volumes of the orthodox Fathers; and when scarcely more than a youth, he lectured publicly on the *De Civitate Dei* of Augustine before a numerous audience, old men and priests not being ashamed to take a lesson in divinity from a young layman, and not at all sorry to have done so. Meantime he applied his whole mind to religion, having some thought of taking orders, for which he prepared himself by watchings and fastings and prayers and such like exercises; wherein he showed much more wisdom than the generality of people, who rashly engage in so arduous a profession without testing themselves beforehand. And indeed there was no obstacle to his adopting this kind of life, except the fact that he could not shake off his wish to marry. Accordingly he resolved to be a chaste husband rather than a licentious priest.

When he married, he chose a very young girl, a lady by birth, with her character still unformed, having been always kept in the country with her parents and sisters,—so that he was all the better able to fashion her according to his own habits. Under his direction she was instructed in learning and in every kind of Music, and had almost completely become just such a person as would have been a delightful companion for his whole life if an early death had not carried her away. She had however borne him several children, of whom three girls, Margaret, Alice and Cecily, and one boy, John, are still living. . . .

His character is entirely free from any touch of avarice. He has set aside out of his property what he thinks sufficient for his children, and spends the rest in a liberal fashion. When he was still dependent on his profession, he gave every client true and friendly counsel with an eye to their advantage rather than to his own, generally advising them, that the cheapest thing they could do was to come to terms with their opponents. If he could not persuade them to do this, he pointed out how they might go to law at least expense; for there are some people whose character leads them to delight in litigation.

In the City of London, where he was born, he acted for some years as judge in civil causes. This office, which is by no means burdensome, —inasmuch as the Court sits only on Thursdays before dinner, —is considered highly honorable; and no judge ever disposed of more suits, or conducted himself with more perfect integrity. In most cases he remitted the fees which are due from the litigants, the practice being for the plaintiff to deposit three groats before the hearing, and the defendant a like sum, and no more being allowed to be exacted. By such conduct he made himself extremely popular in the City.

He had made up his mind to be contented with the position, which was sufficiently dignified without being exposed to serious dangers. He has been thrust more than once into an embassy, in the conduct of which he has shown great ability; and King Henry in consequence would never rest until he dragged him into his Court. "Dragged him," I say, and with reason; for no one was ever more ambitious of being admitted into a Court, than he was anxious to escape it. But as this excellent monarch was resolved to pack his household with learned, serious, intelligent and honest men, he especially insisted upon having More among them, — with whom he is on such terms of intimacy that he cannot bear to let him go. If serious affairs are in hand, no one gives wiser counsel; if it pleases the King to relax his mind with agreeable conversation, no man is better company. Difficult questions are often arising, which require a grave and prudent judge; and these questions are resolved by More in such a way, that both sides are satisfied. And yet no one has ever induced him to accept a present. What a blessing it would be for the world, if magistrates like More were everywhere put in office by sovereigns!

Meantime there is no assumption of superiority. In the midst of so great a pressure of business he remembers his humble friends; and from time to time he returns to his beloved studies. Whatever authority he derives from his rank, and whatever influence he enjoys by the favour of a powerful sovereign, are employed in the service of the public, or in that of his friends. It has always been part of his character to be most obliging to everybody, and marvellously ready with his sympathy; and this disposition is more conspicuous than ever, now that his power of doing good is greater. Some he relieves with money, some he protects by his authority, some he promotes by his recommendation, while those whom he cannot otherwise assist are benefited by his advice. No one is sent away in distress, and you might call him the general patron of all poor people. He counts it a great gain to himself, if he has relieved some oppressed person, made the path clear for one that was in difficulties, or brought back into favour one that was in disgrace. No man more readily confers a benefit, no man expects less in return. And successful as he is in so many ways, —while success is generally accompanied by self-conceit, —I have never seen any mortal being more free from this failing. . . .

However averse he may be from all superstition, he is a steady adherent of true piety; having regular hours for his prayers, which are not uttered by rote, but from the heart. He talks with his friends about a future life in such a way as to make you feel that he believes what he says, and does not speak without the best hope. Such is More, even at Court; and there are still people who think that Christians are only to be found in monasteries! Such are the persons, whom a wise King admits into his household, and into his chamber; and not only admits, but invites, nay, compels them to come in. . . .

You have now before you an ill-drawn portrait, by a poor artist, of an excellent original! You will be still less pleased with the portrait, if you come to have a closer acquaintance with More himself.

ERASMUS [83]

JULY 22

ST. MARY MAGDALEN

It is probable that the unnamed sinner in the Gospel of this day, Mary of Magdalen, and Mary, the sister of Lazarus, are three distinct women. But all these have one trait in common: their attachment to Jesus. In the past because of faulty exegesis the Roman Liturgy, and certain mystics and preachers may have held inexact notions, historically speaking, but they were not mistaken regarding the spiritual realities of humble love and mercy that they invite us to consider.

The liturgy uses the Gospel of the sinful but repentant women again both during Lent (Saturday, Third week) and on the Ember Friday of September.

117

Many sins are forgiven her, for she has loved much. (Gospel)

There is a third, my brethren, there is an illustrious third in Scripture, whom we must associate with these two great Apostles, when we speak of the saints of penance and love. Who is it but the loving Magdalen? Who is it so fully instances what I am showing, as *the woman who was a sinner* [Lk. 7, 37], who watered the Lord's feet with her tears, and dried them with her hair, and anointed them with precious ointment? What a time for such an act! She, who had come into the room as if for a festive purpose, to go about an act of penance! It was a formal banquet, given by a rich Pharisee, to honour, yet to try, our Lord. Magdalen came, young and beautiful, and *rejoicing in her youth, walking in the ways of her heart and the gaze of her eyes:* she came as if to honour that feast, as women were wont to honour such festive doings, with her sweet odours and cool unguents for the forehead and hair of the guests. And he, the proud Pharisee, suffered her to come, so that she touched not him; let her come, as we might suffer inferior animals to enter our apartments, without caring for them; suffered her as a necessary embellishment of the entertainment, yet as having no soul, or as destined to perdition, but anyhow as nothing to him. He, proud being, and his brethren like him, might *compass sea and land to make one proselyte* [Mt. 23, 15]; but, as to looking into that proselyte's heart, pitying its sin, and trying to heal it, this did not enter into the circuit of his thoughts. . . . But, lo, a wondrous sight! was it a sudden inspiration, or a mature resolve? was it an act of the moment, or the result of a long conflict?—but behold, that poor, many-coloured child of guilt approaches to crown with her sweet ointment the head of Him to whom the feast was given; and see, she has stayed her hand. She has looked, and she discerns the Immaculate, the Virgin's Son, *the brightness of the Eternal Light, and the spotless mirror of God's majesty.* [Wis. 7, 26] She looks, and she recognizes the Ancient of Days, the Lord of life and death, her Judge; and again she looks, and she sees in His face and in His mien a beauty, and a sweetness, awful, serene, majestic, more than that of the sons of men, which paled all the splendour of that festive room. Again she looks, timidly yet eagerly, and she discerns in

118

His eye, and in His smile, the loving-kindness, the tenderness, the compassion, the mercy of the Saviour of man. She looks at herself, and oh! how vile, how hideous is she, who but now was so vain of her attractions!—how withered is that comeliness, of which the praises ran through the mouths of her admirers!—how loathsome has become the breath, which hitherto she thought so fragrant, savouring only of those seven bad spirits which dwell within her! And there she would have stayed, there she would have sunk on the earth, wrapped in her confusion and in her despair, had she not cast one glance again on that all-loving, all-forgiving Countenance. He is looking at her: it is the Shepherd looking at the lost sheep, and the lost sheep surrenders herself to Him. He speaks not, but He eyes her; and she draws nearer to Him. Rejoice, you Angels, she draws near, seeing nothing but Him, and caring neither for the scorn of the proud, nor the jests of the profligate. She draws near, not knowing whether she shall be saved or not, not knowing whether she shall be received, or what will become of her; this only knowing that He is the Fount of holiness and truth, as of mercy, and to whom should she go, but to Him who hath the words of eternal life? . . . Wonderful meeting between what was most base and what is most pure! Those wanton hands, those polluted lips, have touched, have kissed the feet of the Eternal and He shrank not from the homage. And as she hung over them, and as she moistened them from her full eyes, how did her love for One so great, yet so gentle, wax vehement within her, lighting up a flame which never was to die from that moment even for ever! and what excess did it reach, when he recorded before all men her forgiveness, and the cause of it! *Many sins are forgiven her, for she loved much; but to whom less is forgiven, the same loveth less. And He said unto her, Thy sins are forgiven thee; thy faith hath made thee safe, go in peace.* [Lk. 7, 47–50]

JOHN HENRY NEWMAN [84]

You will go forth, Magdalene, into the dust-driven world,
Bearing everywhere about you
The stamp of a consummate chasteness;
Wearing here and there on your person,
About your hands,

Along your throat,
Across your lips,
The invisible and radiant marks
Where the Blood was borne,
The mark of the kiss of the lover
Everywhere bears in the flesh of consummation.

And though the manner of your dying
May not be certified—
Jerusalem, or the Greek cities of the East,
Or as the legend tells
Under the sweet Provencal sky—
There could be no death you had not already died,
Its taste was your finalness,
Your rebeginning,
Of what had been begun on the day of the Death,
The day the eagles paired over Juda,
And the Cross tore a hole in the sky.

BROTHER ANTONINUS [85]

JULY 31
ST. IGNATIUS OF LOYOLA

Once converted from a lax way of life, Ignatius knew only one passion, to know Jesus and to make him loved. As he gathered companions who were eventually to form the Society or Company of Jesus, he prepared them for the spiritual combat by the Spiritual Exercises, a month's retreat which was designed to produce a complete change of heart and mind. The Exercises became not only the spiritual basis of the life of the Society but also the principles upon which much of the modern retreat movement is built.

Ignatius got papal approval for his Order in 1541 and became its "general." He died in 1556.

From an historical point of view, our age, the twentieth century, is more difficult to live in than were ages past. But this is our age; it is an age of momentous change, and therefore also a time of new orientation for Christian living. This is our great opportunity. Certainly, we do not want to overdramatize our life, but at the same time we should not let monotonous everyday life blind us to the great risks involved. Nor should we act as if everything in our life is perfectly self-evident. We should be conscious of the fact that we can only master our life with constantly renewed effort—that life of ours that is so dependent on our good will; but still, we are always a bit afraid of that good will of ours, since we do not know for sure how long it will last.

If we consider the above seriously, then we should like to experience the actuality of the Spiritual Exercises for our own individual situation—and it is only from that situation that one can make the Spiritual Exercises.

The Spiritual Exercises are not a theological system. From a theological point of view, the Spiritual Exercises are nothing but an election or choice: the choice of the means and the concrete way in which Christianity can become a living reality in us. St. Ignatius is only interested in this: that a man place himself before the Lord of the "Kingdom of Christ" and the "Two Standards" and ask: What should I do? What do you want from me according to the sovereignty of your divine will?

This brings us to the problem of the present retreat. Certainly, one can set aside some time in which to reflect on oneself, to be silent, to try to be more recollected and more fervent, to learn how to pray again and make one's prayer more intense—spiritual exercises of this kind are praiseworthy and helpful, but this is not what St. Ignatius had in mind. It seems that an election cannot be imposed on one from the outside, nor, especially, be repeated sincerely once a year. For the historical character of our human existence strives for finality and irrevocability, which, in turn, seem to exclude a constantly renewed election. It might flow from all this that, for us, in this retreat, there is no real question of a basic decision for or against God, or the choice of a vocation. But are we so sure that our past decision was truly honest, and not just apparently so? Occasionally, certainly not always, it can be advisable to enter once again into one's own election-situation in order to examine its genuineness.

But this is even more important: Our finite freedom can never embrace the totality of our life in one act. Thus, every decision that we make leaves room for further decisions, which, to be sure, are conditioned and determined by those that have gone before, but are not simply a linear extension of them. Hence, in our yearly retreat we find ourselves in an election-situation. And we can see it, if we will only move aside the debris of our everyday life.

In our annual retreat, therefore, instead of choosing a way of life, we will ourselves with regard to some concrete point: What does God want from me now? Is He pleased by the way I make my meditation, choose my reading material, and so forth? What about my determination to make progress in the spiritual life? We only begin to make a retreat when we have found such an Archimedean point in our lives. In this regard, no retreat master can tell me precisely what God is asking of me. St. Ignatius presupposes that God says to each and every one in a very personal way where his or her election should begin. That is a shocking presupposition! It says that God himself manifests to the retreatant—going beyond whatever is presented by the retreat master—what only He can manifest. Ignatius knows well that each man cannot properly build up his own life from the publicly revealed propositions. Certainly, these propositions are very important. But St. Ignatius believes that God says to each and every man—beyond his own personal reflections on the matter: I want that and that particular thing from you! If I have the courage and the vitality to believe (something that I can never accomplish with my own powers) that God will say something to me during this retreat that I will never be able to disregard in the future, then my retreat could really be Ignatian. That will only come to pass, however, if God is ready. But even the self-preparation and the waiting to see if God will act are worth the trouble.

KARL RAHNER [86]

August

ST. DOMINIC

*Dominic (1170–1221) was the man who understood and trans-
mitted into action the reforming views of the IV Council of the
Lateran (1215 A.D.) and of the papacy at the beginning of the
thirteenth century. In his directives of November 17, 1206, to his
legates charged with combating the Cathar heresy, Pope Innocent III had insisted on the importance of their preaching the
poverty and humility of Christ by word and by example.*

*Beginning as a missionary among the Cathars of the south of
France, Dominic gathered disciples who were to out-do, if possible, the heretics in their asceticism and to engage in a life of
prayer and theological study which would both inflame their zeal
and enlighten their understanding. His companions were to seek
"Truth" (the motto of the Order of Preachers) and what they
penetrated and assimilated of divine truth they were to transmit
to the world in their lectures and their sermons (Contemplata
aliis tradere).*

His mother call'd him Dominic.
And I speak of him, as the laborer,
Whom Christ in his own garden chose to be
His help-mate. Messenger he seem'd, and friend
Fast-knit to Christ; and the first love he show'd,
Was after the first counsel that Christ gave. . . .
But for the real manna, soon he grew
Mighty in learning; and did set himself
To go about the vineyard, that soon turns
To wan and wither'd, if not tended well;
And from the see (whose bounty to the just
And needy is gone by, not through its fault,
But his who fills it basely) he besought,
No dispensation for commuted wrong,
Nor the first vacant fortune, nor the tenths
That to God's paupers rightly appertain,
But, 'gainst an erring and degenerate world,
License to fight, in favor of that seed

From which the twice twelve cions gird thee round.
Then, with sage doctrine and good-will to help,
Forth on his great apostleship he fared,
Like torrent busting from a lofty vein;
And, dashing 'gainst the stocks of heresy,
Smote fiercest, where resistance was most stout.
Thence many rivulets have since been turn'd,
Over the garden catholic to lead
Their living waters, and have fed its plants

DANTE [87]

Lest an immersion in study dry up the emotional side of human nature and dampen the apostolic spirit, Dominic insisted upon the choral office and bodily austerities as essential to his Preaching Brothers.

To begin with, there was to be the full cycle of the chanted Office . . . for he was a great lover of liturgical prayer. The biographers of his life tell us repeatedly of his own fashion in devotion. The morning Mass he sang whenever he possibly could, arranging his journeys in such wise that he could be certain of staying at some priory, whether of his own Order or not, in time for the celebration of the sacred mysteries. We read of him genuflecting countless times before the figure of the crucified, repeatedly prostrating himself *in venia* in the presence of the Blessed Sacrament. Bowing, kneeling, standing, every posture of the body, every gesture of it, had, according to his idea, to be welded into the proper method of addressing God. By nature intensely positive, he looked on the worship to be rendered to God as something which claimed the whole of man, which was due from every gift or faculty of soul or body. Hence the idea of serried ranks of men in choir-stalls, chanting the praises of their maker, and elaborating their ceremony by the detailed and punctilious customs of courts, always held his fancy. He is described to us as leaving his stall and passing up and down among the brethren and exhorting them: *Fortiter, fratres*—"More bravely, my brothers"—so he came to look upon Office said publicly as having a formative effect upon the apostle. It was to make him conscious that he was

125

not alone in his huge and adventurous undertaking, that behind him lay a fighting force of prayer. He was trained to look upon his success as achieved not by the mere convincing tones of his eloquence or the elaborate logic of his argument, but by that far more subtle, more intimate, more supernatural weapon, the power of prayer. Out in the plain where the battle raged men cast back their eyes for courage to the hills, and beheld the forms of angel-hosts carrying up before the throne of the Most High the chants of their fellow-friars. Moreover, in a democracy or at least elective form of government there is the danger of a coarsening of the fibres, men who choose their own superiors are likely to lose some of the due reverence for authority, are, indeed, in grave peril of losing their appreciation even of reverence or veneration. Finally, the critical spirit is certain to be enormously strengthened by the mere development of scholastic ideals. The man of culture, especially the clever, brilliant man (the type chiefly prevalent among the earlier friars), the quick preacher, the ready arguer, the swift dialectician, are all liable from their very trade to have scant respect for tradition or for grave dignity or the calm peace of soul. The restless enquiring Aristotle was far more surely to become the patron saint of preachers than the graver and more contemplative Plato.

To avert, therefore, this calamity and to give weight and measure to what else might be simply shallow talk—scientific, perhaps, but not in any sense rich or harmonious—St. Dominic was led back to the steadying and deepening practice of the choral Office. It makes, when chanted measuredly, the character unconsciously grave and decorous, gives it opportunity for prolonged contemplation of the mysteries and words of God, and affords it that food for daily sustenance which has nowadays to be provided in the form of set meditation. In those days, to lay and cleric, the Divine Office and the sacred service completed the fulness of the matter of the spiritual life. Retreats, meditations, private devotions, were not thought much of in comparison with that official salutation of the Creator.

BEDE JARRETT [88]

AUGUST 6
THE TRANSFIGURATION OF OUR LORD

Peter, James and John are present at the Transfiguration of Christ and they *see his glory* in the midst of Moses and Elijah who also appear in "glory." Jesus is there revealed as the glory of God Himself, dwelling in the midst of His own people. Christ appears here as the glory of God such as filled the tent of meeting where the Ark of the Covenant reposed. The second Epistle of Peter recalls the event thus: *For when he received honor and glory from God the Father and the voice spoke to him from the majestic glory, "This is my beloved Son with whom I am well pleased," we heard this voice borne from Heaven for we were with Him on the holy mountain.* [2 Pet. 1, 17–18] There is here an allusion to Sinai, the holy mountain; there also, the cloud covered the mountain and the glory of the Lord covered Mount Sinai under its shadow (Greek: "descended upon"), and continued thus for six days. [Ex. 24, 15. 16] Peter sets the Transfiguration in relation to the relevation of Sinai, and Luke (and the other Evangelist) in relation to God's appearing upon the tent of meeting. In the two cases Christ is the glory of God, that is to say the Beloved Son, in whom dwells the whole love of the Father.

Peter, in the Gospel account, shows the link between the glory of God manifested and the tent of meeting; he wishes to cover this glory and give it a dwelling-place: . . . *let us therefore make three tabernacles, one for thee, one for Moses and one for Elijah.* The glory of God is present on the earth in the presence of the one who is transfigured and the two who are glorified; the cloud then intervenes as a sign of the Presence of God above them all: *Whilst he spoke there came a cloud and it covered them under its shadow [episkiazein] and, when they entered into the cloud, the disciples were seized with fear, and a voice came forth from the cloud saying: This is my beloved Son; hear him.* [Lk. 9, 34. 35] It is the same verb, "to cover under his shadow" (*ēpiskiazein*) which is used in the book of Exodus, for the tent of meeting as the dwelling-place of the glory. [Ex. 40, 35] In the account of the Annunciation of Mary, the dwelling of the glory, the Son of God, and in the account of the Transfiguration of Christ, the

127

glory of God that Peter would like to put under a tent, thus revealing himself as a Jew eager to respect the law of Moses, the luminous cloud is the sign of the presence of the Father who speaks from on high of His beloved Son, whom He has chosen to be the glory present upon the earth.

It is therefore the same theme which we find in the three accounts of the Exodus, of the Annunciation, and of the Transfiguration, the cloud, the symbol of God's revealed presence which covers with His shadow, and the glory, the symbol of the presence of God, which fills, inhabits and transfigures the place or the being in whom He is. In the first, the glory comes to fill the dwelling-place of God, the tent of meeting; in the second, the holy Son of God comes to inhabit Mary, the new dwelling-place of glory; and in the third the glory reveals itself on the mountain to the eyes of the disciples from without: it has no need of a dwelling-place ('Peter did not understand what he was saying' in his desire to set it under a tabernacle, as was the case with the Ark in the desert). It is at once the Temple and the God who inhabits it, the Son of God who is manifested to the eyes of all, the "full revelation" of His Presence, and the total "unveiling" of the glory. The veil of the Temple will be torn asunder when Christ is crucified to signify the definite emergence of the glory from the Holy of Holies by the resurrection which will bring back Christ for all the world.

The Word became flesh, wrote St. John, *and became "tabernacled" amongst us, and we have seen his "glory," the glory as of the only Son of the Father, "full" of grace and truth.* [Jn. 1, 14] This text once more echoes the classical words of the revealing of God in the Old Testament, in the Annunciation, and in the Transfiguration. The flesh which the Son of God takes at His Incarnation is the new tent, or tabernacle, which the glory is to inhabit, the fullness of grace and truth in our midst. God is truly in the midst of men without any other temple than His Body which radiates His glory, and which His disciples have seen. There is no longer a veil apart from the veil of His flesh which the eye of faith can pierce in order to adore the glory.

MAX THURIAN [89]

128

Today you have manifested on Mount Tabor, O Lord, the glory of your divine image to the chosen of your Apostles, Peter, James, and John; for when they saw your garments glistening as light, and your grace surpassing the sun in splendour, and they could no more bear to behold your unbearable radiance, they fell to the ground, utterly unable to gaze upon it; and they heard a voice from on high testifying and saying, This is my beloved Son, who came into the world to save men.

BYZANTINE LITURGY [90]

AUGUST 8

ST. JOHN VIANNEY

It would be hard to imagine a simpler life than that of John Vianney. Pastor of a small French village for some forty years, he succeeded in converting it from apathy and indifference to a truly fervent Christian life by means of his preaching, prayer, and penance. In addition, he became so widely known for his extraordinary ministry as a confessor and as a spiritual director that a remarkable, perpetual pilgrimage began to Ars. For years he passed most of his days and nights in the confessional and finally literally died of overwork and strain.

He was a priest and pastor par excellence and has been proclaimed the patron saint of all parish priests. "God never seemed so close to us," said those who knew him.

John Vianney and the Eucharist.

The devotion to prayer of St. John M. Vianney, who was to spend almost the whole of the last thirty years of his life in church caring for the crowds of penitents who flocked to him, had one special characteristic—it was specially directed toward the Eucharist. It is almost unbelievable how ardent his devotion to Christ hidden beneath the veils of the Eucharist really was. "He is the one," he said, "who has loved us so much; shouldn't we love Him in return?" He was devoted to the adorable Sacrament of the altar with a burning charity and his soul was drawn

129

to the sacred tabernacle by a heavenly force that could not be resisted. This is how he taught his faithful to pray: "You do not need many words when you pray. We believe on faith that the good and gracious God is there in the tabernacle; we open our souls to Him; and feel happy that He allows us to come before Him; this is the best way to pray." He did everything that there was to be done to stir up the reverence and love of the faithful for Christ hidden in the sacrament of the Eucharist and to bring them to share in the riches of the divine Synaxis; the example of his devotion was ever before them. To be convinced of this—witnesses tell us—all that was necessary was to see him carrying out the sacred rites or simply see him genuflect when he passed the tabernacle.

JOHN XXIII [91]

If man knew his religion.

Neither wealth, nor honors, nor vanity can make a man happy during his life on earth, but only attachment to the service of God, when we are fortunate enough to realize that and to carry it out properly. The woman who is held in contempt by her husband is not unhappy in her state because she is held in contempt but because she does not know her religion or because she does not practice what her religion tells her she should do. Teach her her religion, and from the moment that you see her practice it, she will cease to complain and to consider herself unhappy. Oh! How happy man would be, even on this earth, if he knew his religion! . . .

What power that person who is near to God possesses when he loves Him and serves Him faithfully! Alas, my dear brethren, anyone who is despised by worldly people, who appears to be unimportant and humble, look at him when he masters the very will and power of God Himself. Look at Moses, who compels the Lord to grant pardon to three hundred thousand men who were indeed guilty. Look at Josue, who commanded the sun to stand still and the sun became immobile, a thing which never happened before and which perhaps will never happen again. Look at the Apostles: simply because they loved God, the devils fled before them, the lame walked, the blind saw, the dead arose to life. Look at St. Benedict, who commanded the rocks to stop in their course and they remained hanging in mid-air. Look at him who multiplied bread, who made water come out of rocks, and who disposed of the stones and the forest as easily as if they were wisps of straw. Look at a St. Francis of Paula who commands the fish to come to hear the word of God and they respond to his call with such loyalty that they applaud his words. Look at a St. John who commands the birds to keep silent and they obey him. Look at many others who walk the seas without human aid. Very well! Now take a look at all those impious people and all those famous ones of the world with all their wit and all their knowledge for achieving everything. Alas! Of what are they really capable? Nothing at all. And why not? Unless it is because they are not attached to the service of God. But how powerful and how happy at the same time is the person who knows his religion and who practices what it commands.

Alas, my dear brethren, the man who lives according to the direction of his passions and abandons the service of God is both unhappy and capable of so little! Put an army of one hundred thousand men around a dead man and let them employ all their power to bring him back to life. No, no, my dear children, he will not come to life again. But let someone who is despised by the world, but who enjoys the friendship of God, command this dead man to take up life again; immediately you will see him arise and walk. We have other proofs of this, too. If it were necessary to be wealthy or to be very learned to serve God, a great many people would be unable to do it. But, no, my dear children, extensive learning or great wealth are not at all necessary for the service of God. On the contrary, they are often a very big obstacle to it. Yes, my dear brethren, let us be rich or poor, in whatever state we may be, learned or otherwise, we can please God and save our souls. . . .

Listen to me for one moment and you will see that only the service of God will console us and make us happy in the midst of all the miseries of life. To accomplish it, you do not need to leave either your belongings, or your parents, or even your friends, unless they are leading you to sin. You have no need to go and spend the rest of your lives in the desert to weep there for your sins. If that were necessary for us, indeed, we should be very happy to have such a remedy for our ills. But no, a father and a mother of a family can serve God by living with their children and bringing them up in a Christian way. A servant can very easily serve God and his master, with nothing to stop him.

No, my dear brethren, the way of life which means serving God changes nothing in all that we have to do. On the contrary, we simply do better all the things we must do.

ST. JOHN VIANNEY [92]

AUGUST 10
ST. LAWRENCE

The deacon Lawrence was one of the most illustrious martyrs of the Roman Church, dying during the persecution of the emperor Valerian (258 A.D.). Ordered to surrender the funds set aside for the poor, he refused and was punished in exemplary fashion.

The examples of the noble deaths of the Lacedaemonians and others scarce touch us. For what good is it to us? But the example of the death of the martyrs touches us; for they are "our members." We have a common tie with them. Their resolution can form ours, not only by example, but because it has perhaps deserved ours. There is nothing of this in the examples of the heathen. We have no tie with them; as we do not become rich by seeing a stranger who is so, but in fact by seeing a father or a husband who is so.

BLAISE PASCAL [93]

This day is renowned because of the martyr Lawrence's crown of baptism. No part of the Roman world is ignorant of the merits of this outstanding martyr. He suffered in the very capital of the nations, that is, in the city of Rome itself. For he ministered there as a deacon, and there in the flower of his youth he purpled his youthful beauty with his blood. His suffering is extraordinary and much to be admired. With the Lord's help, I shall briefly narrate it.

He was an archdeacon when Blessed Sixtus [II] was bishop, whose triumphal martyrdom occurred three days earlier. When the holy Lawrence was following his bishop, Sixtus, on his way to martyrdom, he was sustained by his faith and sad at heart —not because Sixtus was about to suffer, but because he himself was being left behind by the bishop. Sixtus, the venerable old man, looked back at the youth and said: "Do not be sad, my son. You will follow me three days from now." After Lawrence heard this prophecy, he was soon fully prepared in his heart and intoxicated with spiritual joy. He had hope that what he who knew had predicted would certainly come to pass.

After a while, he was seized and led away. Since he was an archdeacon, he was believed to have the resources of the Church in his possession. The persecutor desired to get these, motivated more by anger than by avarice. He hated the man he was putting to death, but in him he admired his attitude of contempt. However, the holy Lawrence was poor in goods, but rich in virtues. He did not deny that he had the riches of the Church, but requested a delay of three days in order to display them. Thereupon he ordered groups of the poor to be assembled. When he was summoned to his trial on the very day he won his crown, as if he were about to display what his judge wanted, he showed what he had. The persecutor asked: "Where are the riches of the Church?" But Lawrence extended his hand toward the poor and said: "These are the riches of the Church."

He spoke what was true, but bitter. Is it strange if this truth increased the hatred? Angry over being ridiculed, the cruel tyrant and avaricious enemy, who perhaps would have thought up a penalty less severe, ordered his men to kill the admirable young man by the sword and to prepare flames. He was afire himself rather than setting fire to another. He was applying fire to another's flesh, but blazing in his own heart. And his torture was as much more serious as it was interior.

Next, some one brought out the well-known gridiron for martyring Lawrence by parching him—or, to speak more truly, by roasting him. He was bound fast by iron, but he regarded that gridiron of torture as a bed of rest. I used the word torture. It was torture according to the mind of the torturer, but not according to the outlook of the victim. There is no torture of a condemned

133

man where there is not a penalty for sin. Consequently, the most blessed martyr, showing how quietly he was resting on that red-hot iron, told the bystanders: "Turn me over now. If one side is cooked, begin to eat."

We admire his patience. Let us admire this as a gift of God. In this case his faith was not burning painfully in him; it was even consoling the man who was being roasted. Why was faith consoling him? Because it was keeping faithful the One making promises. God was bestowing on Lawrence all these as His gifts: that his faith might not fail, that his hope might not be quenched, that his charity might be enkindled the more amid his bodily punishments of fire.

ST. PETER CHRYSOLOGUS [94]

AUGUST 15
THE ASSUMPTION OF MARY

On November 1, 1950, after consulting the bishops of the world, Pope Pius XII felt it opportune to define as a dogma the traditional belief of the Church in the bodily assumption of Mary.

We are confident that this solemn proclamation and definition of the Assumption will contribute in no small way to the advantage of human society, since it redounds to the glory of the Most Blessed Trinity, to which the Blessed Mother of God is bound by such singular bonds. It is to be hoped that all the faithful will be stirred up to a stronger piety towards their heavenly Mother, and that the souls of all those who glory in the Christian name may be moved by the desire of sharing in the unity of Jesus Christ's Mystical Body and of increasing their love for her who shows her motherly heart to all the members of this august Body. And so we may hope that those who meditate upon the glorious example Mary offers us may be more and more convinced of the value of a human life entirely devoted to carrying out the heavenly Father's will and to bringing good to others. Thus, while the illusory teachings of materialism and the corruption of morals that follows from these teachings threaten to extinguish the light of virtue and to ruin the lives of men by exciting discord among them, in this magnificent way all may see clearly to what a lofty goal our bodies and souls are destined. Finally it is our hope that belief in Mary's bodily Assumption into heaven will make our belief in our own resurrection stronger and render it more effective. . . .

For which reason, after We have poured forth prayers of supplication again and again to God, and have invoked the light of the Spirit of Truth, for the glory of Almighty God Who has lavished His special affection upon the Virgin Mary, for the honor of her Son, the immortal King of the Ages and the Victor over sin and death, for the increase of the glory of that same august Mother, and for the joy and exultation of the entire Church; by the authority of Our Lord Jesus Christ, of the Blessed Apostles Peter and Paul, and by Our own authority, We pronounce, declare, and define it to be a divinely revealed dogma: that the Immaculate Mother of God, the ever Virgin Mary, having completed the course of her earthly life, was assumed body and soul into heavenly glory.

PIUS XII [95]

The whole history of salvation of the one human race is a single tremendous drama. We have already said that by the coming of the Word of God into the world, this sacred history has already entered its final phase, that a factor has already been established in this history which—though the lot of the individual may still be undecided—stamps it in its totality with the mark of finality. For the decisive truth of Christian faith is that the Lord is truly risen. And since it is in our humanity, in our flesh and blood, that he has risen, been glorified and taken up into the glory of his Father, that fundamental doctrine of Christianity proclaims from the start, that eternal glory is even now a possibility in the history of this world, this humanity and this flesh; already a possibility because in the flesh of Christ, which is a part of this world, it is already a reality.

Now faith tells us that Mary is the perfect achievement and work of redemption, and that this perfection of her grace has entered its final stage, because she has left this earthly life of space and time, and entered the phase of her life in which no new events take place in freedom as on earth, but the harvest sown within the confines of time is gathered into God's eternity. Mary,

135

however, in her life on this earth was the highest, unmatched realization of redemption in a human being endowed with grace, as mother of God and consequently as the perfect type or representative of redemption in its very essence. And she has already attained her perfect beatitude—no one can doubt this, who believes that she, sinless and full of grace, has accomplished her earthly course. Furthermore, in the chronology of sacred history the hour is already far advanced, so that in principle, perfect attainment of perfection and beatitude in soul and body is already possible—this cannot be doubted either, by anyone who believes that Christ is risen with his human nature. Consequently, faith, coming to full awareness of its own content, cannot but confess what the Church defined: After the completion of her earthly life, Mary was assumed body and soul into the glory of heaven.

KARL RAHNER [96]

AUGUST 20
ST. BERNARD OF CLAIRVAUX

Such was his influence on it that men have called the twelfth century the age of St. Bernard (1090–1153). In addition to being the abbot-founder of the great abbey of Clairvaux, which soon came to number seven hundred monks, and the founder of sixty-five other Cistercian abbeys, Bernard preached the II Crusade, mediated between popes, kings, and bishops, preached widely, wrote voluminously, healed a papal schism, worked for the reform of the clergy, and engaged in the significant polemical battles of his age.

As a doctor of the Church he is particularly important for his devotion to the Sacred Humanity of Christ and to the Blessed Virgin Mary, and for his theology of the mystical ascent to God through acquired and infused contemplation.

Bernard describes the Cistercian way.

Our *Ordo,* our observance, is to be under a Master, under an Abbot; under a rule, under discipline. Our *Ordo* is the practice of silence, exercise in fasting, vigils, prayers; manual labor. *But above all it is to hold to the more excellent way,* which is charity, and indeed to progress in all these things from day to day, and to persevere in them until the last day.

ST. BERNARD OF CLAIRVAUX [97]

Seeking after God.

It is a great good to seek God. I think that, among all the blessings of the soul, there is none greater than this. It is the first of the gifts of God; the last degree of the soul's progress. By no virtue is it preceded; to none does it give place. To what virtue is that added which is not preceded by any? And to which should that give way which is the consummation of all virtues? For what virtue can be ascribed to him who is not seeking God, or what limit prescribed to one who is seeking him? *Seek his face evermore,* says the psalmist [Ps. 104, 4]; nor do I think that when a soul has found him, it will cease from seeking. God is sought, not by the movement of the feet, but by the desires of the heart; and when a soul has been so happy as to find him, that sacred desire is not extinguished, but, on the contrary, is increased. Is the consummation of the joy the extinction of the desire? It is rather to it as oil poured upon a flame; for desire is, as it were, a flame. This is, indeed, the case. The joy will be fulfilled; but the fulfillment will not be the ending of the desire, nor therefore of the seeking. But think, if you can, of this earnest love of seeking God as being without any deprivation of him, and of the desire for him as without anxiety or trouble of mind. His presence excludes the one, and the abundance of his graces prevents the other.

But now observe why I have made these introductory remarks. It is that every soul among you that is seeking God should know that it has been anticipated by him, and has been sought by him before it began to seek him. For without this knowledge it might

137

be that out of a great blessing might arise great harm, if, when it has been filled with the good gifts of the Lord, it treats those gifts as if they had not been received from him, and so does not render to God the glory of them. It is, doubtless, in this way that some who appeared very great before men, because of the graces which had been conferred upon them, were counted as the least before God, inasmuch as they did not render back to him the glory which was due on their account. . . .

By night on my bed I sought him whom my soul loves. [Cant. 3, 1] The soul seeks the Word, but it had been previously sought by the Word. For otherwise, when it had been once driven out or cast forth from the presence of the Word, it would have returned no more to obtain the sight of the good things it had lost if it had not been sought by the Word. Our soul, if abandoned to itself, is a spirit which goes to and fro, but does not return. Listen to a fugitive and wandering soul, and learn what it complains of, and what it seeks: *I have gone astray like a lost sheep: seek thy servant.* [Ps. 118, 176] O man, dost thou desire to return? But if that depends upon thy own will, why dost thou entreat help? Why dost thou ask for from another what thou hast in abundance in thy own self? It is plain that he does desire this, and is not able to perform it; he is a spirit which goes to and fro, and returns not; though he who has not even the wish to return is farther removed still. Yet I would not say that the soul which longs to return, and desires to be sought, is wholly exposed and abandoned. For from whence comes this willingness which is in it? It comes, if I do not mistake, from its having been already sought and visited by the Word; nor is that visitation fruitless, since it has so worked in the soul as to produce that good will without which a return would not be possible. But it does not suffice to be sought once only, so great is the languor of the soul, and so great the difficulty of the return. What if the will of a soul is to return? The will lies inoperative if it be not supported by the power to do so. For, *To will is present with me,* says the apostle, *but how to perform that which is good I find not.* [Rom. 7, 18] What is it, then, that the psalmist seeks in the passage that I have quoted? He plainly seeks nothing else than to be sought: which he would not seek if he had been sought sufficiently. This latter grace, indeed, is what he entreats: *Seek thy servant;* that is, that what it has been granted to him to desire it may be granted to him also perfectly to attain, according to the good pleasure of God.

ST. BERNARD OF CLAIRVAUX [98]

AUGUST 24

ST. BARTHOLOMEW

Let us consider the particular praise which our Saviour gives him. *Behold an Israelite indeed, in whom is no guile!* [Jn. 2, 47] This is just the character which (through God's grace) they may attain most fully, who live out of the world in the private way I have been describing, —which is made least account of by man, and thought to be in the way of success in life, though our Saviour chose it to make head against all the power and wisdom of the world. Men of the world think an ignorance of its ways is a disadvantage of disgrace; as if it were somehow unmanly and weak to have abstained from all acquaintance with its impieties and lax practices. How often do we hear them say that a man must do so and so, unless he would be singular and absurd; that he must not be too strict, or indulge high-flown notions of virtue, which may be good to talk about, but are not fit for this world! When they hear of any young person resolving on being consistently religious, or being strictly honest in trade, or observing a noble purity in language and demeanour, they smile and think it very well, but that it will and must wear off in time. And they are ashamed of being innocent, and pretend to be worse than they really are. Then they have all sorts of little ways—are mean, jealous, suspicious, censorious, cunning, insincere, selfish; and think others as low-minded as themselves, only proud, or in some sense hypocritical, unwilling to confess their real motives and feelings.

To this base and irreligious multitude is opposed the Israelite indeed, in whom there is no guile. David describes his character in the fifteenth Psalm; and, taken in all its parts, it is a rare one. He asks, *Lord, who shall abide in Thy tabernacle? who shall dwell in Thy holy hill? He that walketh uprightly, and worketh righteousness, and speaketh the truth in his heart. He that backbiteth not with his tongue, nor doeth evil to his neighbour, nor taketh up a reproach against his neighbour. In whose eyes a vile*

139

person is contemned; but he honoureth them that fear the Lord.
He that sweareth to his own hurt, and changeth not.

I say, it is a difficult and rare virtue, to mean what we say, to love without dissimulation, to think no evil, to bear no grudge, to be free from selfishness, to be innocent and straightforward. This character of mind is something far above the generality of men; and when realized in due measure, one of the surest marks of Christ's elect. And the instances which we may every now and then discover of it among Christians, will be an evidence to us, if evidence be wanting, that, in spite of all that grovelling minds may say about the necessity of acquaintance with the world and with sin, in order to get on well in life, yet after all, inexperienced guilelessness carries a man on as safely and more happily. For, first, it is in itself a great privilege to a rightly disposed mind, not to be sensible of the moral miseries of the world; and this is eminently the lot of the simple-hearted. They take everything in good part which happens to them, and make the best of every one; thus they have always something to be pleased with, not seeing the bad, and keenly sensible of the good. And communicating their own happy peace to those around them, they really diminish the evils of life in society at large, while they escape from the knowledge of them themselves. Such men are cheerful and contented; for they desire but little, and take pleasure in the least matters, having no wish for riches and distinction. And they are under the tyranny of no evil or base thoughts, having never encouraged what in the case of other men often spreads disorder and unholiness through their whole future life. They have no phantoms of former sins, such as remain even to the penitent, when he has subdued their realities, rising up in their minds, harassing them, for a time domineering, and leaving a sting behind them. Guileless persons are, most of all men, skilful in shaming and silencing the wicked; —for they do not argue, but take things for granted in so natural a way, that they throw back the sinner upon the recollection of those times of his youth, when he was pure from sin, and thought as they do now; and none but very hardened men can resist this sort of appeal. Men of irreligious lives live in bondage and fear; even though they do not acknowledge it to themselves. Many a one, who would be ashamed to own it, is afraid of certain places or times, or of solitude, from a sort of instinct that he is no company for good spirits, and that devils may then assail him. But the guileless man has a simple boldness and a princely heart; he overcomes dangers which others shrink from, merely because they are no dangers to him, and thus he often gains even worldly advantages, by his straightforwardness, which the most crafty persons cannot gain, though they risk their souls for them.

JOHN HENRY NEWMAN [99]

AUGUST 28
ST. AUGUSTINE

His conversion.

And now from my hidden depths my searching thought had dragged up and set before the sight of my heart the whole mass of my misery. Then a huge storm rose up within me bringing with it a huge downpour of tears. So that I might pour out all these tears and speak the words that came with them I rose up from Alypius (solitude seemed better for the business of weeping) and went further away so that I might not be embarrassed even by his presence. This was how I felt and he realized it. No doubt I had said something or other, and he could feel the weight of my tears in the sound of my voice. And so I rose to my feet, and he, in a state of utter amazement, remained in the place where we had been sitting. I flung myself down on the ground somehow under a fig tree and gave free rein to my tears; they streamed and flooded from my eyes, an acceptable sacrifice to Thee. And I kept saying to you, not perhaps in these words, but with this sense: *And Thou, O Lord, how long? How long, Lord; wilt Thou be angry forever? Remember not our former iniquities.* [Ps. 6, 3; 12, 1; 78, 8] For I felt that it was these which were holding me fast. And in my misery I would exclaim: "How long, how long this 'tomorrow and tomorrow'? Why not now? Why not finish this very hour with my uncleanness?"

So I spoke, weeping in the bitter contrition of my heart. Suddenly a voice reaches my ears from a nearby house. It is the voice of a boy or a girl (I don't know which) and in a kind of singsong the words are constantly repeated: "Take it and read it. Take it and read it." At once my face changed, and I began to think carefully of whether the singing of words like these came into any kind of game which children play, and I could not remember that I had ever heard anything like it before. I checked the force of my tears and rose to my feet, being quite certain that I must interpret this as a divine command to me to open the book and read the first passage which I should come upon. For I had heard this about Antony: he had happened to come in when the Gospel was being read, and as though the words read were spoken directly to himself, had received the admonition: *Go, sell all that thou hast, and give to the poor, and thou shalt have treasure in heaven, and come and follow me.* [Mt. 19, 21] And by such an oracle he had been immediately converted to you.

So I went eagerly back to the place where Alypius was sitting, since it was there that I had left the book of the Apostle when I rose to my feet. I snatched up the book, opened it, and read in silence the passage upon which my eyes first fell: *Not in rioting and drunkenness, not in chambering and wantonness, not in strife and envying: but put on the Lord Jesus Christ, and make not provision for the flesh in concupiscence.* [Rom. 13, 13–14] I had no wish to read further; there was no need to. For immediately I had reached the end of this sentence it was as though my heart was filled with a light of confidence and all the shadows of my doubt were swept away.

ST. AUGUSTINE [100]

The love of God.

There is no doubt in my mind, Lord, that I love you. I feel it with certainty. You struck my heart with your word, and I loved you. But, see, *heaven and earth and all that therein is* on every side are telling me to love you, and they never stop saying it to all men, *that they may be without excuse.* [Rom. 1, 20] But more deeply *wilt Thou have mercy on whom Thou wilt have mercy, and wilt*

142

have compassion on whom Thou hast had compassion [Rom. 9, 15]; otherwise heaven and earth are telling your praises to deaf ears.

But what do I love when I love you? Not the beauty of the body nor the glory of time, not the brightness of light shining so friendly to the eye, not the sweet and various melodies of singing, not the fragrance of flowers and unguents and spices, not manna and honey, not limbs welcome to the embraces of the flesh: it is not these that I love when I love my God. And yet I do love a kind of light, melody, fragrance, food, embracement when I love my God; for He is the light, the melody, the fragrance, the food, the embracement of my inner self—there where is a brilliance that space cannot contain, a sound that time cannot carry away, a perfume that no breeze disperses, a taste undiminished by eating, a clinging together that no satiety will sunder. This is what I love when I love my God.

And what is this God? I asked the earth and it answered: "I am not he," and all things that are on the earth confessed the same. I asked the sea and the deeps and the creeping things with living souls, and they replied: "We are not your God. Look above us." I asked the blowing breezes, and the universal air with all its inhabitants answered: "Anaximenes was wrong. I am not God." I asked the heaven, the sun, the moon, the stars, and "No," they said, "we are not the God for whom you are looking." And I said to all those things which stand about the gates of my senses: "Tell me about my God, you who are not He. Tell me something about Him." And they cried out in a loud voice: "He made us." My question was in my contemplation of them, and their answer was in their beauty.

ST. AUGUSTINE [101]

Late it was that I loved you, beauty so ancient and so new, late I loved you! And, look, you were within me and I was outside, and there I sought for you and in my ugliness I plunged into the beauties that you have made. You were with me, and I was not with you. Those outer beauties kept me far from you, yet if they had not been in you, they would not have existed at all. You called, you cried out, you shattered my deafness: you flashed,

143

you shone, you scattered my blindness: you breathed perfume, and I drew in my breath and I pant for you: I tasted, and I am hungry and thirsty: you touched me, and I burned for your peace.

ST. AUGUSTINE [102]

September

St. Peter Claver
The Holy Cross
St. Cyprian of Carthage
St. Matthew the Evangelist
The Jesuit Martyrs
St. Michael and all Angels
St. Jerome

SEPTEMBER 9
ST. PETER CLAVER

St. Peter Claver [1580–1654] is one of the greatest glories of the Society of Jesus. He is not one of the intellectual saints like St. Robert Bellarmine and St. Peter Canisius, or a great administrator like St. Ignatius Loyola or St. Francis Borgia. His place is among the missionaries of genius: Francis Regis, Francis di Girolamo, and especially with St. Francis Xavier. The Council of Tarragona named Claver the "Apostle of the West Indies" as Xavier was called "Apostle of the East Indies." The parallel is unavoidable. Both were unwearying in zeal, both baptized more than 300,000 pagans. Xavier was the wandering apostle opening new roads to the Church. Claver was the apostle who stayed in one spot. The former sought out souls along the routes of his journeys: to the latter souls came as to a safe harbor. In their methods both were revolutionaries, though Claver was more of a traditionalist than Xavier, and more of a disciple. They were holy sociologists, who taught without a plan of campaign and carried through an immense operation. Xavier freed the east and ended its isolation from Europe, Claver converted to Christ the Africans who came to the New World. . . .

Claver was born in an heroic age, an epic age, an age when the task was to consolidate and absorb a new world, both physically and morally. He was born into a country that was living through its golden age. It was an environment full of the problems of conquest, of a search for *El Dorado*. Sacrifices were readily made in both causes. Deeds which appear to us today heroic even in saints were carried out by soldiers as part of their normal duty. There appeared to be a competition in tenacious courage between sword and cross. The thirst for material glory produced military and political geniuses, and the thirst for souls produced a company of saints. The heroism and courage of Pizarro, Cortes, Magallanes, Quesada and Almagro were mirrored in the heroism of the missionaries. Loyola, St. Teresa and Claver sought the conquest of the new world of the spirit, spurred on by the errors of heresy, the growing moral laxity or pagan ignorance.

In Claver there was a powerful reaction against the cruelty of this expanding world. If the slavers and plantation owners could live in Cartagena and Africa, putting up with heat and epidemics, why should not the apostle of Christ do likewise? This reaction against man's cruelty to man was a mainspring of his activity. What Father Las Casas was for the Indian, Sandoval and Claver were for the Negro. Sandoval always refused to recognize the lawfulness of the slave-trade. It is idle to seek for moderation and sweet reasonableness in a man who witnessed the abject misery of these human beings treated as brute beasts. In his environment Claver was an extremist in fearless love. He was a man of his times. He lived his life in the greatest slave-port the world had then seen, and he lived there within the Jesuit mission which specialized in the apostolate to the Negro. There is not in ecclesiastical history a case of a man who has brought into the Church through baptism so many non-white pagans. A million slaves passed through Cartagena, and before they went on their way to Portobello, Quito, Lima and other places to the south, one-third of them came into contact with Claver. . . .

Wherever there were slaves, in the mines and the plantations, there were some who had heard from his lips a word of love and redemption, who wore a medallion given to them by their friend in Cartagena.

For three reasons Claver deserves the proud title of "Liberator of a Race". First, because as these poor wretches landed in Cartagena, their faces reflecting their terror, he was able to offer them in the midst of their abandonment the joy of sensing that they were individuals, and human. Second, because by making himself—a white man—the slave of black men, he showed that there exists a fundamental equality in men behind all appearances. This ideal was to be the seed of the future incorporation of their successors into Christian nations. And third, because not merely with words, but with the sacrifice of his own life, he proved that pity and love still remained in the world, and that they might reduce the load of hatred placed on each slave by so much injustice.

Through his tremendous and heroic sacrifice Peter Claver brought into the seventeenth-century world the message of the redemption of the poor through love. After 300 years this message has its tasks to perform today. There are still millions of

147

slaves, with no brand on their arms, but the mark of slavery in their tyrannized souls. Many spiritual liberators are needed, slaves to sacrifice themselves for the modern bondsman. . . .

St. Peter Claver did not only wish to *relieve* the Negro slave: he wished to *redeem* him also. But St. Peter Claver did not justify useless rebellion and bloodshed for his Negro slaves, his mission was not to be a Spartacus but an apostle who devoted himself passionately heart and soul to that race. Mildness for him was not a timid compromise but a creed. Exaggeration and violence were not necessary to his purpose. To the slave-traders he turned a sad and serious face. His slavery to the slaves was the greatest reproach to those who considered themselves their masters. Had St. Peter Claver not possessed that mildness which has been condemned, he would not have baptized 300,000 brothers: he would have failed if he had put weapons in his Negroes' hands, he would not have been the liberator of a race but its exterminator. The decrees of political liberty which followed eventually would not have been possible in a society which had not been prepared for it by the Gospel.

ANGEL VALTIERRA [103]

In modern America Martin Luther King continues Claver's energetic apostolate of love and nonviolence.

There will be no permanent solution to the race problem until oppressed men develop the capacity to love their enemies. The darkness of racial injustice will be dispelled only by the light of forgiving love. For more than three centuries American Negroes have been battered by the iron rod of oppression, frustrated by day and bewildered by night by unbearable injustice, and burdened with the ugly weight of discrimination. Forced to live with these shameful conditions, we are tempted to become bitter and to retaliate with a corresponding hate. But if this happens, the new order we seek will be little more than a duplicate of the old order. We must in strength and humility meet hate with love.

Of course, this is not *practical*. Life is a matter of getting even, of hitting back, of dog eat dog. Am I saying that Jesus commands us to love those who hurt and oppress us? Do I sound like most preachers—idealistic and impractical? Maybe in some distant Utopia, you say, that idea will work, but not in the hard, cold world in which we live.

My friends, we have followed the so-called practical way for too long a time now, and it has led inexorably to deeper confusion and chaos. Time is cluttered with the wreckage of communities which surrendered to hatred and violence. For the salvation of our nation and the salvation of mankind, we must follow another way. This does not mean that we abandon our righteous efforts. With every ounce of our energy we must continue to rid this nation of the incubus of segregation. But we shall not in the process relinquish our privilege and our obligation to love. While abhorring segregation, we shall love the segregationist. This is the only way to create the beloved community. To our most bitter opponents we say: "We shall match your capacity to inflict suffering by our capacity to endure suffering. We shall meet your physical force with soul force. Do to us what you will, and we shall continue to love you. We cannot in all good conscience obey your unjust laws, because noncooperation with evil is as much a moral obligation as is cooperation with good. Throw us in jail, and we shall still love you. Bomb our homes and threaten our children, and we shall still love you. Send your hooded perpetrators of violence into our community at the midnight hour and beat us and leave us half dead, and we shall still love you. But be ye assured that we will wear you down by our capacity to suffer. One day we shall win freedom, but not only for ourselves. We shall so appeal to your heart and conscience that we shall win *you* in the process, and our victory will be a double victory."

MARTIN LUTHER KING [104]

SEPTEMBER 14

THE EXALTATION OF THE HOLY CROSS

This liturgical solemnity has several historical origins, commemorating as it does: the discovery of the holy cross by St. Helena, mother of the emperor Constantine; the consecration of the Basil-

ica of the Resurrection, containing both Calvary and the empty tomb; and finally the triumphant return of the relic of the true cross from Persian captivity by the emperor Heraclius in 630.

On this feast the Church wishes us to contemplate not so much the sufferings of Christ in themselves but rather the joys they procure us and the glory which results from them, for Christ and for all the members of his body. "Through it we are saved and set free." (Introit)

On the splendor and the power of the cross.

Wherever the symbol of the Cross is set up, Christ's victory and the devil's subjection are signified. You know that our old enemy won his victory over the first man by means of a tree, and because of that held him and all his issue . . . under the yoke of his tyranny. But the Son came, as a strong man to the race, that He might strive with the powers of the air, and to that first tree opposed another, spewing out through the bitterness of the Cross the poisonous delight of the apple of old. When the first man, tempted by Satan, stretched out his hand to the tree, it was as if he wrote the bond of his unconditional servitude on wooden tablets. But the second Adam, stretching out His hands on the Cross, obliterated the bond of that deadly agreement. By a tree then we were enslaved; by a tree also we have been restored to our pristine freedom. By a tree we were cast out from Paradise; by a tree we are called once more to our native land. And we who because of a tree were regarded as enemies have by the mystery of the Cross been restored to friendship with God and concord with the angels, as the Apostle bears witness, when he speaks of Christ to the Ephesians: *For he is our peace, who has made both one, and has broken down the middle wall of partition: having abolished in his flesh the enmity, making void even the law of commandments contained in ordinances; for to make in himself of twain one new man, so making peace, and that he might reconcile both unto God in one body by the Cross, having slain the enmity thereby* [Eph. 2, 14–17]. . . .

This emblem of heavenly triumph, by which the world was loosed from the bonds of her ancient captivity, was adored by the

Fathers from the world's beginning, and foretold by the Prophets and prefigured on every page of the Holy Scriptures. That which we adore in grace, they venerated in faith. And we now see fulfilled, by the grace of the Mediator, what was prefigured to them in enigmas; what they predicted in spirit we can behold and embrace with our bodily eyes. O wonderful loving-kindness of our Creator! O praiseworthy humility of our Redeemer! He deigned to suffer the pains of a most cruel death, that He might win for us a crown. He chose of His own will, the dreadful torments of the Cross in order to raise us from the yoke of slavery to the kingdom. He did not scorn to be cursed, so that He might free us from the law's curse. He suffered a shameful death to deliver us from the disgrace of everlasting death. So the Apostle says: *Christ has redeemed us from the curse of the law, being made a curse for us; for it is written: Cursed is every one that hangs on a tree; that the blessing of Abraham might come on the Gentiles through Jesus Christ; that we might receive the promise of the Spirit through faith* [Gal. 3, 13–14]. . . .

We must mark and most diligently consider, brethren, that our Redeemer first passed over by the Cross and so raised His humanity to the glory of the right hand of the Father. In doing so He gave us an example: where the head goes, the members must follow. We are signed with the Cross on our foreheads; it will avail even more to our salvation if we hold it in our hearts. When the angel of death saw *both* doorposts smeared with blood, he passed by instead of bursting in. Let no one rely on the mark of the cross on his forehead if he does not show forth the truth of the Cross in his works. St. Paul showed forth the Cross in his behaviour most notably, and said: *I bear in my body the marks of the Lord Jesus.* [Gal. 6, 17]

Therefore, dearly beloved, let us cleanse ourselves from all defilement of body or spirit; let us arm ourselves to break the assault of our enemies, the vices, let us counteract the passions of carnal pleasure, and minister lovingly to the needs of our neighbours and suffer injuries in a spirit of charity. Let our souls be free from all the burdens of earthly greeds, so that, hurled on wings of holy desire they may forsake the depths and returning to their Maker rest sweetly in His love. Let us despise all that we see and hasten with unceasing labour to that which we believe. This in-

151

deed is the cross which we must imprint on all our actions, all our behaviour. This is the Cross which we are commanded to bear after the Lord daily. He who carries it truly shares in the passion of his Redeemer. This emblem will separate the sheep from the goats in the last judgement. And the judge, who knows not the wicked, will recognize this mark in His own. Those whom He sees marked with the seal of His own death He will, as a gracious rewarder, invite to partake in the prize of everlasting life: *Come, He will say, blessed of my Father, inherit the kingdom* [Mt. 25, 34] of Him with whom He Himself lives and reigns for ever and ever. Amen.

ST. PETER DAMIAN [105]

The cruciform.

Everything reminds us of the cross. We ourselves are made in the form of a cross. Balm and sweetness exhale from the cross. The unction which overflows from the cross inundates our souls in proportion as we unite ourselves with it, holding it tightly against our hearts. The cross contains more wisdom than any book; all who do not know this book are ignorant, however many other books they may have studied. Those only are truly wise who love and consult this book, who study it deeply. Bitter as this book is, they are never happier than when they can immerse themselves in its bitterness. The more they frequent this school, the more they desire to remain there; never do their studies weary them.

ST. JOHN VIANNEY [106]

SEPTEMBER 16
ST. CYPRIAN OF CARTHAGE

This great bishop of Carthage and primate of North Africa can be numbered among the Church's most illustrious converts from paganism. Cyprian himself has described the marvel of his baptismal transformation: "The regenerating waters washed away the stains of my former life; a great light from on high shed its rays in my purified heart; the Spirit falling from heaven changed

152

me into a new man by means of a second birth. At that very instant, in the most marvelous manner, certitude succeeded doubt, once closed doors opened before me, and light shone in darkness; I found easy what before had appeared hard and possible what I had believed impossible."

One of the great defenders and expanders of Christian faith and order in the third century, he suffered banishment and then martyrdom in the Decian persecution of 258. He had spoken of martyrdom with eloquence. "Who," wrote St. Robert Bellarmine, "can read Cyprian attentively, without feeling himself set on fire with a love of martyrdom."

An exhortation to martyrdom.

We must all stand prepared for the battle; nor consider anything but the glory of life eternal, and the crown of the confession of the Lord; and not regard those things which are coming as being such as were those which have passed away. A severer and a fiercer fight is now threatening, for which the soldiers of Christ ought to prepare themselves with uncorrupted faith and robust courage, considering that they drink the cup of Christ's blood daily, for the reason that they themselves also may be able to shed their blood for Christ. For this is to wish to be found with Christ, to imitate that which Christ both taught and did, according to the Apostle John, who said, *He that says he abides in Christ, ought himself to walk even as He walked* [1 Jn. 2, 6]. . . .

The Lord desired that we should rejoice and leap for joy in persecutions, because, when persecutions occur, then are given the crowns of faith, then the soldiers of God are proved, then the heavens are opened to martyrs. For we have not in such a way given our name to warfare that we ought only to think about peace, and draw back from and refuse war, when in this very warfare the Lord walked first—the Teacher of humility, and endurance, and suffering—so that what He taught to be done, He first of all did, and what He exhorts to suffer, He himself first suffered for us. . . .

For the secular contest men are trained and prepared, and reckon it a great glory of their honour if it should happen to them to be crowned in the sight of the people, and in the presence of the emperor. Behold a lofty and great contest, glorious also with the reward of a heavenly crown, inasmuch as God looks upon us as we struggle, and, extending His view over those whom He has condescended to make His sons, He enjoys the spectacle of our contest. God looks upon us in the warfare, and fighting in the encounter of faith; His angels look on us, and Christ looks on us. How great is the dignity, and how great the happiness of the glory, to engage in the presence of God, and to be crowned, with Christ for a judge! Let us be armed, beloved brethren, with our whole strength, and let us be prepared for the struggle with an uncorrupted mind, with a sound faith, with a devoted courage. Let the camp of God go forth to the battle-field which is appointed to us. Let the sound ones be armed, lest he that is sound should lose the advantage of having lately stood; let the lapsed also be armed, that even the lapsed may regain what he has lost: let honour provoke the whole; let sorrow provoke the lapsed to the battle. The Apostle Paul teaches us to be armed and prepared, saying, *We wrestle not against powers, and the princes of this world and of this darkness, against spirits of wickedness in high places. Wherefore put on the whole armour, that you may be able to withstand in the most evil day, that when you have done all you may stand; having your loins girt about with truth, and having put on the breastplate of righteousness; and your feet shod with the preparation of the Gospel of peace; taking the shield of faith, wherewith you shall be able to quench all the fiery darts of the wicked one; and the helmet of salvation, the sword of the Spirit, which is the word of God.* [Eph. 6, 12–17]

Let us take these arms, let us fortify ourselves with these spiritual and heavenly safeguards, that in the most evil day we may be able to withstand, and to resist the threats of the devil: let us put on the breastplate of righteousness, that our breast may be fortified and safe against the darts of the enemy: let our feet be shod with evangelical teaching, and armed, so that when the serpent shall begin to be trodden and crushed by us, he may not be able to bite and trip us up: let us bravely bear the shield of faith, by the protection of which, whatever the enemy darts at us may be extinguished: let us take also for protection of our head the helmet of salvation, that our ears may be guarded from hearing the deadly edicts; that our eyes may be fortified, that they may not see the odious images; that our brow may be fortified, so as to keep safe the sign of God; that our mouth may be fortified, that the conquering tongue may confess Christ its Lord: let us also arm the right hand with the sword of the Spirit, that it may bravely reject the deadly sacrifices; that, mindful of the Eucharist, the hand which has received the Lord's body may embrace the Lord Himself, hereafter to receive from the Lord the reward of heavenly crowns.

ST. CYPRIAN [107]

SEPTEMBER 21
ST. MATTHEW THE EVANGELIST

Matthew gave up a comfortable living to follow Christ.

According to the rule of the Gospel, the absence of wealth is, as such, a more blessed and a more Christian state than the possession of it.

The most obvious danger which worldly possessions present to our spiritual welfare is, that they become practically a substitute in our hearts for that One Object to which our supreme devotion is due. They are present; God is unseen. They are means at hand of effecting what we want: whether God will hear our petitions for those wants is uncertain; or rather I may say, certain in the negative. Thus they minister to the corrupt inclinations of our nature; they promise and are able to be gods to us, and such gods too as require no service, but, like dumb idols, exalt the worshipper, impressing him with a notion of his own power and security. And in this consist their chief and most subtle mischief. Religious men are able to repress, nay extirpate sinful desires, the lust of the flesh and of the eyes, gluttony, drunkenness, and the like, love of amusements and frivolous pleasures and display, indulgence in luxuries of whatever kind; but as to wealth, they cannot easily rid themselves of a secret feeling that it gives them a footing to stand upon, an importance, a superiority; and in consequence they get attached to this world, lose sight of the duty of bearing the Cross, become dull and dim-sighted, and lose their delicacy and preci-

155

sion of touch, are numbed (so to say) in their fingers' ends, as regards religious interests and prospects. To risk all upon Christ's word seems somehow unnatural to them, extravagant, and evidences a morbid excitement; and death, instead of being a gracious, however awful release, is not a welcome subject of thought. They are content to remain as they are, and do not contemplate a change. They desire and mean to serve God, nay actually do serve Him in their measure; but not with the keen sensibilities, the noble enthusiasm, the grandeur and elevation of soul, the dutifulness and affectionateness towards Christ which become a Christian, but as Jews might obey, who had no Image of God given them except this created world, *eating their bread with joy, and drinking their wine with a merry heart, caring that their garments be always white, and their head lacking no ointment, living joyfully with the wife whom they love all the days of the life of their vanity, and enjoying the good of their labour.* [Eccl. 9, 7–9, 18] Not, of course, that the due use of God's temporal blessings is wrong, but to make them the object of our affections, to allow them to beguile us from the "One Husband" to whom we are espoused, is to mistake the Gospel for Judaism.

JOHN HENRY NEWMAN [108]

The Christian moral revolution overturns so many accepted ethical values that it is difficult to see how much of a rational structure of law based on nature could be left. Rational morality is the code by which man uses the goods of self and of this world in a way suitable to man living in society. The gospel does not so much reject secular goods as ignore them. The words of Jesus on wealth scarcely allow any room for a morality of the use of these goods. I have already noticed that the primitive community took him seriously. Does their failure to find a practical way to follow his teaching excuse other Christians from looking for a way? It is not without design that Matthew begins his account of the teaching of Jesus with the words, *Blessed are the poor in spirit*—a phrase nicely mistranslated for hundreds of years. It means those who are poor of spirit, who have not much spirit, the helpless of the world who have no power to resist. The gospel was proclaimed to the poor whose masses constituted the vast majority of the Hellenistic world, and it was proclaimed by one of them. He did not offer riches but congratulated them on their poverty.

JOHN L. MCKENZIE [109]

SEPTEMBER 26
THE JESUIT MARTYRS OF NORTH AMERICA

The story of these missionary martyrs is "truly one of the most austere, the most onerous, the most excruciating, and yet one of the most momentous apostolic labors in the history of the Catholic missions." The educational products of the Christian humanism of the Jesuit colleges, these refined French gentlemen worked patiently and joyfully in the savage squalor of the Huron villages and then laid down their lives for the sake of the infant Church they had founded.

Fathers John de Brébeuf, Gabriel Lallemant, Charles Garnier, Noël Chabanel, and Anthony Daniel were done to death in Canada (1648–1649); Father Isaac Jogues and the lay oblates René Goupil and John de la Lande were martyred in what is now upper New York state (1642–1646).

The martyrdom of Fathers John de Brébeuf and Gabriel Lallemant in Huronia, March 16 and 17, 1649.

We had been informed by some escaped captives of the certain deaths of Fathers Jean de Brébeuf and Gabriel Lallemant. The next morning as soon as we were assured that the enemy had departed we sent one of our Fathers and seven other Frenchmen to seek their bodies at the place of torture. There they found a spectacle of horror—the remains of cruelty personified—or, rather, the testimony of the love of God which alone triumphs in the death of martyrs. . . .

As soon as they were taken captive they were stripped naked and some of their nails torn out. The welcome which they received upon entering the village of Saint-Ignace was a hailstorm of blows with clubs on their shoulders, their loins, their legs, their chests, their abdomens, and their faces—no part of their bodies escaped suffering its own torment.

Father Jean de Brébeuf, overwhelmed by the burden of these blows, did not for all that disregard the care of his flock. Seeing himself surrounded by Christans whom he himself had instructed and who were now suffering captivity with him, he encouraged them thus: "My children, let us raise our eyes to heaven in the midst of our unutterable afflictions; let us remember that God is witness to our sufferings and that he will soon be our glorious reward. Let us die in this faith and let us hope from his goodness the fulfillment of his promises. I feel much more pity for you than for myself. Bear with courage the few remaining torments. They will end with our lives, but the glory which follows them will never end." *"Echon"* (this is the name which the Hurons gave to Father Brébeuf), they replied, "our spirits will be in Heaven while our bodies are still suffering on earth. Pray to God for us, that he may show us his mercy; we will invoke him until death."

Some Huron infidels—former captives of the Iroquois and now naturalized among them, long-standing enemies of the Faith— were annoyed by these words and by the fact that the Fathers, though their captives, did not hold their tongues captive. They cut off the hands of one and pierced the other with sharp awls and iron points. They applied hatchets heated red in the fire to their armpits and to their loins. They placed a necklace of these glowing ax heads about their necks in such a way that any motion of their bodies produced a new torture. If they attempted to lean forward, the red-hot iron hanging behind them burned their shoulders, and if they thought they could avoid that pain by bending back a little, their chests and stomachs suffered a similar torment. If they stood upright, without leaning to one side or the other, these glowing hatchets touched them on all sides and were an intolerable torment to them. Their persecutors fastened on them belts of bark filled with pitch and resin, then set them afire and thus burned the entire body of their poor victims.

At the height of these torments Father Gabriel Lallemant raised his eyes to heaven, clasped his hands several times, and sent prolonged sighs to God, begging his aid. Father Jean de Brébeuf suffered like a rock, insensible to the fires and the flames, not uttering a single cry, but keeping a profound silence. This restraint thoroughly astonished his tormentors. No doubt the heart of the sufferer was already reposing in his God. Then, as if returning to himself, he preached to those infidels, his torturers. He had more encouragement, however, for the many good Christian captives who felt a deep sympathy for him.

His persecutors then became indignant at his zeal, and to hinder him from speaking further of God, they gouged out circles around his mouth, cut off his nose, and tore off his lips. His blood then spoke more loudly than his lips had done. Since his heart was not yet torn out, his tongue did not fail to serve him until his last sigh, blessing God for all these torments and exhorting his Christians more vigorously than ever.

In derision of holy baptism which these good Fathers had so charitably administered even during the attack and in the heat of the fight, those wretched enemies of the Faith devised the plan of baptizing the Fathers with boiling water. Their charred bodies were completely bathed in it, not only once, but two or three times, and even more, with biting insults to accompany these torments. "We baptize you," announced these heathens, "so that you may be blessed in Heaven, for without proper baptism you cannot be saved." Others mockingly added: "We treat you as a friend, since we are the cause of your greatest happiness in Heaven. Thank us for our kind services, for the more you suffer the more your God will reward you."

Most of these tormentors were apostate Hurons who had been captives among the Iroquois for a long period and were longtime enemies of the Faith. They had had sufficient instruction for their salvation but had impiously abused it. Truly their cruelty did serve for the glory of the Fathers, but it is much to be feared that it was also for their own ignominy. . . .

Their tortures were not of the same duration. Father Jean de Brébeuf was at the height of his agony at about three o'clock on the same day he was captured, March 16. He rendered up his soul about four o'clock in the evening. Father Gabriel Lallemant suffered longer, from six o'clock in the evening until about nine o'clock the next morning, March 17 [1649].

Before they died, both of them had their hearts torn out by means of an opening above the breast. Those inhuman barbarians feasted on these organs, drinking the blood of their victims while it was still quite warm, drawing it from its source with sacrilegious hands. While the Fathers were living and still conscious, pieces of flesh were removed from their thighs and from the calves of their legs. These morsels their executioners placed on coals to roast and then ate them in the sight of their captives.

The torturers had slashed the holy bodies of the Fathers in various places, and in order to increase their pain had thrust red-hot hatchets into their wounds.

Father Jean de Brébeuf had had the covering of his skull torn away; his feet were cut off and the flesh torn from his thighs all the way down to the bone. A hatchet blow had split one of his jaws.

Father Gabriel Lallemant had received a hatchet blow on the left ear, driving it all the way into his brain and clearly exposing this latter organ. We could find no part of his body, from his feet to his head, which had not been broiled and scorched while he was still alive—even his eyes, into which those impious wretches had thrust burning coals.

They had broiled the tongues of both saints, repeatedly thrusting flaming fire-brands and burning pieces of bark into their mouths to prevent them from invoking even while dying him for whom they were suffering and who could never die in their hearts. I have learned all these details from persons worthy of credence. They saw it and reported it to me first-hand. These men had been the fellow captives of our Fathers, but, having been reserved for death at a later date, had managed to escape.

PAUL RAGUENEAU [110]

SEPTEMBER 29

ST. MICHAEL AND ALL ANGELS

Angels are derived from that first light which is without beginning, for they possess the power of illumination; and they have no need of tongue or hearing, for without a word exchanged between them they communicate their thoughts and counsels with one another. They are created by the Word, and by the sanctification of the Holy Spirit are they brought to perfection, and each shines in brightness and grace according to his value and his place in God's sight. Also, they are circumscribed: for when they are in Heaven they are not on earth and when they are sent by God on earth they do not remain in Heaven. They are not hemmed in by walls and doors, by locks and seals, for they have unlimited powers. I say they have unlimited powers because, when God wished them to appear before worthy men and reveal themselves, then they assume the shape the beholder is capable of seeing. Yet that alone is perfectly unlimited which is uncreated, and every created thing is limited by God who created it. . . .

They are mighty and prompt to fulfill the desires of God, and they are endowed with such speed that wherever the divine will bids them go, there they are straightway found. They are the guardians of the divisions of the earth; they are set over the nations and regions allotted to them by God; they govern all our affairs and bring us succor. And the reason surely is that they are set over us by the divine will and command and are ever in the neighborhood of God.

ST. JOHN OF DAMASCUS [111]

Angels also are inhabitants of the world invisible, and concerning them much more is told us than concerning the souls of the faithful departed, because the latter rest from their labours; but the Angels are actively employed among us in the Church. They are said to be *ministering spirits, sent forth to minister for them who shall be heirs of salvation.* [Heb. 1, 14] No Christian is so humble but he has Angels to attend on him, if he lives by faith and love. Though they are so great, so glorious, so pure, so wonderful, that the very sight of them (if we were allowed to see them) would strike us to the earth, as it did the prophet Daniel, holy and righteous as he was; yet they are our fellow-servants and our fellow-workers, and they carefully watch over and defend even the humblest of us, if we be Christ's. That they form a part of our unseen world, appears from the vision seen by the patriarch Jacob. We are told that when he fled from his brother Esau, *he lighted upon a certain place, and tarried there all night, because the sun had set; and he took of the stones of that place, and put them for his pillows, and lay down in that place to sleep.* [Gen. 28, 11] How little did he think that there was any thing very wonderful in this spot! It looked like any other spot. It was a lone, uncomfortable place: there was no house there: night was coming on; and he had to sleep upon the bare rock. Yet how different was the truth! He saw but the world that is seen; he saw not the world that is not seen; yet the world that is not seen was there. It was there, though it did not at once make known its presence, but needed to be supernaturally displayed to him. He saw it in his sleep. *He dreamed, and behold, a ladder set up on the earth, and the top of it reached up to heaven; and behold, the Angels of God ascending and descending on it. And behold, the Lord stood above it.* [Gen. 28, 12] This was the other world. Now, let this be observed. Persons commonly speak as if the other world did not exist now, but would after death. No: it exists now, though we see it not. It is among us and around us. Jacob was shown this in his dream. Angels were all about him, though he knew it not. And what Jacob saw in his sleep, that Elisha's servant saw as if with his eyes; and the shepherds, at the time of the Nativity, not only saw, but heard. They heard the voices of those blessed spirits who praise God day and night, and whom we, in our lower state of being, are allowed to copy and assist.

JOHN HENRY NEWMAN [112]

SEPTEMBER 30
ST. JEROME

What survives and impresses modern Christians of this fourth-century Latin Father (347–420) is his devotion to and service in behalf of the Bible. When his controversial works and his ardent —and sometimes uncharitable—polemics have been largely forgotten, the fact that he devoted half a life-time to translating the Hebrew and Greek Scriptures brings him near to our times when the Bible is once again becoming the handbook of the Christian.

Preface to "The Dialogue against the Pelagians."

Having written a letter to Ctesiphon, in which I answered the questions that he had raised, I have repeatedly been asked by my brothers why I was putting off any longer the work that I had promised to publish in which I declared that I would answer all of the questions raised by those who preach the doctrine of apathy.* That is, to be sure, the doctrine that was the bone of contention between the Stoics and the Peripatetics, that is to say, the Old Academy; for the one school asserted that *páthé*, which we read in Latin as *perturbationes,* such as sorrow, joy, hope, and fear, could be completely eradicated and extirpated from the minds of men; while the other school held that these disturbances can be restrained and mastered and controlled and kept within proper bounds and checked like bridled horses with certain curbs. Cicero discusses their views in his *Tusculan Disputations* and Origen seeks to blend these views with ecclesiastical truth in his *Stromata,* not to mention Manichaeus, Priscillian, Evagrius of Ibora, Jovinian, and the heretics of practically the whole of Syria, who are erroneously referred to in the pagan tongue as *Massaliani,* and in the Greek as *Euchítes.* All of them assert that human virtue and human knowledge can achieve a perfection, and I do not mean in the sense of a likeness to, but an equality with God, to such a high degree that they hold that, once they have reached the pinnacle of perfection, they cannot commit even sins of thought and ignorance. And although I did discuss in brief manner, due to the press of time, a few of the points in the earlier letter that I sent to Ctesiphon in refutation of their errors, in the present work that I am in the process of composing, I shall follow the method of the Socratics of presenting all the arguments that can be stated by both parties, so that the truth might become more evident, once each side has presented its views. Moreover, it is Origen's own peculiar view that it is impossible for human nature to pass through life without sinning; and, on the other hand, that it is possible for any man, who has changed his life for the better, to gain such strength that he never sins again.

However, I shall say briefly, in reply to those who say that it was the fury of envy that prompted me to write this work, that I have never spared heretics, and have endeavored in every possible manner to make the enemies of the Church my own enemies. Helvidius wrote a treatise against the perpetual virginity of Holy Mary. Was I motivated by envy to reply to a man whom I have

* Apathy is the Stoic doctrine of freedom from passions.

never seen in the flesh? Jovinian, whose heresy is being revived at the present time, shocked the faith of Rome while I was absent from the city, and his language was so inelegant and so abusive that he was more deserving of pity than of envy. I also replied to him to the best of my ability. Rufinus exerted every effort to make available, not only to one city, but to the whole world, the blasphemies of Origen and the books of the *Periarchon,* and went so far as to even publish the first book of Eusebius' *Apology for Origen* under the name of the martyr Pamphilus, and, as if the former had expressed himself unsatisfactorily, he spewed forth a new book in his defense. Am I envious of him because I answered him, and because the flood of his eloquence was so torrential that I lost all desire for writing and dictating? Palladius, a slave to villainy, tried to revive the same heresy and to add fresh insult to my Hebrew translation. Am I envious both of his genius and his nobility? Even now the mystery of evil is at work and everybody expresses freely his personal views; I am the only one to whom the glory of all men is a source of irritation, and my lot is so wretched that I am jealous even to those individuals who do not deserve to be envied. Hence, in order to prove to the whole world that it is not persons that I hate, but rather their errors, and that I am not seeking to bring disgrace upon my brothers, but rather am pitying the lot of those who are being tripped up by what is falsely called knowledge, I have proposed the names of Atticus and Critobulus, using them as the mouthpieces for our own views and those of the adversaries. Nay more, it is the hope and prayer of all of us who profess the Catholic faith that heresy be refuted and individuals be converted. Or, if they choose to persist in error, the blame is certainly not to be placed on us who have written the treatise, but rather on those who have preferred falsehood to truth. And we reply briefly to those calumniators, who impute their own reproaches to those individuals, that it is the view of the Manichaeans to revile the nature of man, and to destroy free will, and to rule out the help of God. And again, that it is a sign of very manifest folly for man to say that he is what God is; and that we must travel the royal road in such a way that we turn neither to the left nor to the right; and that we believe that the cravings of our own will are always guided by the help of God. But if anybody cries out loud that false charges are being brought against him, and boasts that he is in agreement with our views, then, and only then, will he prove that he is in agreement with the true faith, when openly and without guile he condemns the opposite views, lest he hear these words of the prophet said to him: *And after all this, her treacherous sister Juda hath not returned to me with her whole heart, but with falsehood.* (Jer. 3, 10) It is a less serious sin to pursue evil which you assumed was good than to lack the courage to defend what you know for certain is good. We, who cannot bear threats, injury, and poverty, how shall we overcome the fires of Babylon? Let false peace not destroy what war has spared. I do not want to learn perfidy through fear, when Christ has left the true faith up to my own will.

ST. JEROME [113]

October

St. Therese of Lisieux
St. Francis of Assisi
The Motherhood of Mary
St. Teresa of Avila
St. Luke the Evangelist
Sts. Simon and Jude
Christ the King

OCTOBER 3
ST. THERESE OF LISIEUX

This young Carmelite saint (1873–1897) whose spiritual fame spread far and wide immediately after her obscure death in a Norman convent reminds our busy world preoccupied with temporal values of the primacy of the spiritual, of humility and love and prayer.

Spiritual childhood.

As you know, dear Mother, I've always wished that I could be a saint. But whenever I compared myself to the Saints there was always this unfortunate difference—they were like great mountains, hiding their heads in the clouds, and I as only an insignificant grain of sand, trodden down by all who passed by. However, I wasn't going to be discouraged; I said to myself: God wouldn't inspire us with ambitions that can't be realised. Obviously there's nothing great to be made of me, so it must be possible for me to aspire to sanctity in spite of my insignificance. I've got to take myself just as I am, with all my imperfections; but somehow I shall have to find out a little way, all of my own, which will be a direct shortcut to heaven. After all (I said to myself) we live in an age of inventions. Nowadays, people don't even bother to climb the stairs—rich people, anyhow; they find a lift more convenient. Can't I find a lift which will take me up to Jesus, since I'm not big enough to climb the steep stairway of perfection? So I looked in the Bible for some hint about the lift I wanted, and I came across the passage where Eternal Wisdom says: *Is anyone simple as a little child? Then let him come to me.* [Prov. 9, 4] To that Wisdom I went, it seemed as if I was on the right track; what did God undertake to do for the child like soul that responded to his invitation? I read on, and this is what I found: *I will console you like a mother caressing her son; you shall be like children carried at the breast, fondled on a mother's lap.* [Is. 66, 12–13] Never were words so touching: never was such music to rejoice the heart—I could, after all, be lifted up to heaven, in the arms of

Jesus! And if that was to happen, there was no need for me to grow bigger; on the contrary, I must be as small as ever, smaller than ever.

ST. THERESE OF LISIEUX [114]

The power of prayer.

What an extraordinary thing it is, the efficiency of prayer! Like a queen, it has access at all times to the Royal presence, and can get whatever it asks for. And it's a mistake to imagine that your prayer won't be answered unless you've something out of a book, some splendid formula of words, specially devised to meet this emergency. If that were true, I'm afraid I should be in a terribly bad position. You see, I recite the Divine Office, with a great sense of unworthiness, but apart from that I can't face the strain of hunting about in books for these splended prayers—it makes my head spin. There are such a lot of them, each more splendid than the last; how am I to recite them all, or to choose between them? I just do what children have to do before they've learnt to read; I tell God what I want quite simply, without any splendid turns of phrase, and somehow he always manages to understand me. For me, prayer means launching out of the heart towards God; it means lifting up one's eyes, quite simply, to heaven, a cry of grateful love, from the crest of joy or the trough of despair; it's a vast, supernatural force which opens out my heart, and binds me close to Jesus.

ST. THERESE OF LISIEUX [115]

The soul that is enfolded by Divine love can't remain inactive; though it may, like Mary, sit at the feet of Jesus and listen to those words of his, so full of fire, so full of comfort; not appearing to contribute anything, but really contributing so much! More than Martha, as she hurries distractedly to and fro, and wishes her sister would do the same. (Not that our Lord has any fault to find with Martha's exertions; his own Mother, Mother of God though she was, put up with humble work of that kind all her life; didn't she get the meals ready for the Holy Family? Martha is a devoted hostess, but she won't keep calm, that's the trouble.) All the Saints have seen the importance of Mary's attitude, and perhaps particularly the ones who have done most to fill the world with the light of Gospel teaching. Surely those great friends of God, people like St. Paul and St. Augustine and St. John of the Cross and St. Thomas and St. Francis and St. Dominic, all went to prayer to find the secret of their wisdom; a Divine wisdom which has left the greatest minds lost in admiration.

"Give me a lever and a fulcrum," said the man of science, "and I'll shift the world." Archimedes wasn't talking to God, so his request wasn't granted; and in any case he was only thinking of the material world. But the Saints really have enjoyed the privilege he asked for; the fulcrum God told them to use was himself, nothing less than himself, and the lever was prayer. Only it must be the kind of prayer that sets the heart all one fire with love; that's how the Saints shift the world in our own day, and that's how they'll do it to the end of time.

ST. THERESE OF LISIEUX [116]

OCTOBER 4
ST. FRANCIS OF ASSISI

The perfect joy of St. Francis.

One day Saint Francis was travelling from Perugia to Saint Mary of the Angels. It was winter, and he was suffering severely from the bitter cold. And he called to Brother Leo, who was walking a short distance ahead, saying:

"Brother Leo, although the Friars Minor throughout the land are setting a high example of holiness and edification, nevertheless write down and note well that this is not the source of perfect joy." And a little further along the road Saint Francis called out a second time:

"Brother Leo, even though a Friar Minor could give sight to the blind, make the crooked straight, cast out devils, restore hearing to the deaf, make the lame walk and the dumb speak, and even raise to life one who had been dead four days, write down that this is not the source of perfect joy."

And going on a little further, he cried out loudly: "Brother

169

Leo, were a Friar Minor to know every language and every science, and all the scriptures, so that he could foretell and reveal not only the future but even the secrets of the conscience and soul, write down that this is not the source of perfect joy."

Going on a little further, Saint Francis again called out loudly:

"Brother Leo, little lamb of God, even if a Friar Minor could speak with the tongue of an angel, knows the courses of the stars and the properties of herbs; and if all the treasures of the earth were revealed to him, and he understood the ways of birds, fish, and all beasts, of men, of trees, of rocks, of roots, and of waters —write down that this is not the source of perfect joy."

And walking on a little further, Saint Francis called out loudly:

"Brother Leo, even if a Friar Minor were such an eloquent preacher that he could convert all unbelievers to the Faith of Christ, write down that this is not the source of perfect joy."

Saint Francis continued to discourse on this theme for nearly two miles, until Brother Leo in great bewilderment asked him: "Father, I beg you in God's Name, tell me the source of perfect joy!"

And Saint Francis answered him: "When we arrive at Saint Mary of the Angels soaked with rain, stiff with cold, covered with mud, and exhausted with hunger, and we knock at the friary door, and the porter asks angrily, 'Who are you?' and we answer, 'We are two of your brothers,' and he says, 'You are liars. You are a couple of rogues, who wander about deceiving folk and robbing the poor of alms. Be off with you!' and if he refuses to open, and forces us to stand outside all night in the snow and rain, hungry and frozen, then if we bear such ill-treatment, abuse, and dismissal patiently and calmly, without complaint, humbly and charitably thinking that the porter recognizes us for what we are, and that God moves him to denounce us; write down, Brother Leo, that here is the source of perfect joy.

"And if we go on knocking, and he comes out angrily and drives us away as importunate rogues with abuse and blows, saying, 'Be off, you dirty thieves! Go to the poorhouse, for you're not going to eat or lodge here!'; and we bear this patiently, cheerfully, and charitably, Brother Leo, write down that here is the source of perfect joy.

"And if, driven by hunger, cold, and darkness, we continue to knock, begging him with tears to open and admit us for the love of God, and he, more furious than ever, says: "These are persistent rascals! I will give them what they deserve!" and rushes out with a knotted stick, grabs us by our cowls, throws us to the ground, and rolls us in the snow, belabouring us with every knot on his stick; and if we bear this patiently and cheerfully, remembering the sufferings of Christ the Blessed, and how we should bear this for love of Him: Brother Leo, write down that here is the source of perfect joy.

"And now listen to the conclusion, Brother Leo. Above all graces and gifts of the Holy Spirit that Christ gives to His friends is the grace to conquer self, and willingly to bear any pain, injury, insult, and hardship for love of Christ. For we cannot glory in any other gifts of God except these, because they are not ours, but God's. Therefore the Apostle says: *What did you possess that was not given you by God? And if you have received it from Him, why do you glory as though you had it of yourself?* [1 Cor. 4, 7] But in the cross of suffering and affliction we may glory, because this is our own. So the Apostle says: *I will not glory except in the Cross of our Lord Jesus Christ** [Gal. 6, 14], to whom be everlasting honour and glory for ever and ever.

THE FIORETTI [117]

❧

THE SONG OF BROTHER SUN

Most High, Almighty, good Lord,
Thine be the praise, the glory, the honour,
And all blessing.

To Thee alone, Most High, are they due,
And no man is worthy
To speak Thy Name.

Praise to Thee, my Lord, for all Thy creatures,
Above all Brother Sun
Who brings us the day and lends us his light;

* Motto of the Franciscan order.

171

Lovely is he, radiant with great splendour,
And speaks to us of Thee,
O Most High.

Praise to Thee, my Lord, for Sister Moon and the stars
Which Thou hast set in the heavens,
Clear, precious, and fair.

Praise to Thee, my Lord, for Brother Wind,
For air and cloud, for calm and all weather,
By which Thou supportest life in all Thy creatures.

Praise to Thee, my Lord, for Sister Water,
Who is so useful and humble,
Precious and pure.

Praise to Thee, my Lord, for Brother Fire,
By whom Thou lightest the night;
He is lovely and pleasant, mighty and strong.

Praise to Thee, my Lord, for our sister Mother Earth
Who sustains and directs us,
And brings forth varied fruits, and coloured flowers, and plants.

Praise to Thee, my Lord, for those who pardon one another
For love of Thee, and endure
Sickness and tribulation.

Blessed are they who shall endure it in peace,
For they shall be crowned by Thee,
O Most High.

Praise to Thee, my Lord, for our Sister bodily Death
From whom no man living may escape:
Woe to those who die in mortal sin.

Blessed are they who are found in Thy most holy will,
For the second death cannot harm them.

Praise and bless my Lord,
Thank Him and serve Him
With great humility.

ST. FRANCIS [118]

OCTOBER 11
THE MOTHERHOOD OF MARY

The Church never grows tired of celebrating the privileges of Mary. Pope Pius XI established this feast in 1931 to commemorate the vindication of her supreme title Theotókos (Mother of God) by the Ecumenical Council of Ephesus in 431.

We confess, our Lord Jesus Christ, the unique Son of God, perfect God and perfect man, of a reasonable soul and body; begotten of the Father before the ages according to the Godhead, the same in the last days for us and for our salvation born of Mary the Virgin according to the manhood; the same consubstantial with the Father in Godhead, and consubstantial with us in manhood, for a union of two natures took place; therefore we confess one Christ, one Son, one Lord. According to this understanding of the unconfused union we confess the holy Virgin to be *theotókos,* because God the Word was made flesh and lived as man, and from the very conception united to himself the temple taken from her. As to the evangelical and apostolic phrases about the Lord, we know that theologians treat some in common, as of one person, and distinguish others, as of two natures, and interpret the God-befitting ones in connection with the Godhead of Christ, and the humble ones of the manhood.

COUNCIL OF EPHESUS [119]

Christianity is a new life, an eternal life, that is brought to men, and they are born to this life during the whole time of their earthly existence. But since it is their life, it is a human life, and human life requires a maternal principle as well as a paternal principle.

This is why God has created that marvel of marvels which is the heart of mothers. He has placed in it a deep, obstinate, and, we may even say, an unreasonable love, a love ready for all sacrifices, all eventualities, all favoritisms. What would become of us poor creatures if, during the years of our helplessness and misery, someone who is made for love did not bend over us, and if we did not have the certitude, anchored in our blood, that we are dear to someone? . . .

God did not intend that supernatural life should be less human than natural life; quite the contrary. Nor did He wish the children He adopts in His Son to be left half-orphans.

So He Created the Blessed Virgin. He who instills marvels of tenderness into the hearts of ordinary mothers could not fail to instill the same love into the heart of this pre-eminent mother, whose love for her only Son and for her adopted sons was to be in some fashion the counterpart of His own love. In her heart we shall find heaped-up miracles of affection and sweetness, something mysterious like the life of grace to which they correspond and like the Incarnation which is their inspiration.

For, to repeat, the Incarnation is everything; but its completeness is brought out by its gift of the Mother of God to men, so that she is their mother through a supernatural motherhood. If God Himself has made a virgin a mother, and if He has wished that she who is the mother of the God-man should also be the mother of the human race, He would not inspire her with motherly feelings of a tepid and reserved kind that would not be enough for even an ordinary mother.

The divine maternity, as St. Thomas says, belongs to the order of infinite things; consequently the maternal love it expresses is in some sense infinite. Mother of the Infinite, mother in whom this infinite Son becomes the life of all mankind, she is to be, in a way, infinitely a mother, and God gives her a heart great enough to love correspondingly. We are here dealing with something that is meant seriously and sincerely, with all the realism of the Incarnation. . . .

In the designs of Providence there is an aspect of Christ's love that men do not see clearly unless they look at His mother, just as there is an aspect of God's love that men do not see clearly unless they look at the God-man. . . .

Where this sweet mother of grace is lacking, God Himself does not stand forth so convincingly as a Father, Christ is not so close to us, the Church is less of a family society, and Christianity loses much of its gracious charm. . . .

In the order of love and donation which is Christianity, Christ glories in living for the benefit of all men. The same is true of His mother. Her high prerogatives do not cause estrangement, but open up possibilities of goodness and close union for all men; they are the expression of a Catholic function and a universal service. A service, to be sure; has not Jesus come to serve? Do not mothers have the great and sovereign right of being, in their touching way, the servants of their children? *Behold the handmaid of the Lord*—and of the Son, and of the Lord's sons.

EMILE MERSCH [120]

So now we must consider that this holy virgin became the mother of Jesus Christ our Lord and saviour; the fact that Mary is the mother of God. As the reflection of the Church, guided by her faith, attained a more and more explicit awareness and expression of the divine sonship of our Lord and saviour Jesus, and of the unity of his divine person despite—and in—the duality of natures, human and divine, it was correspondingly certain from the first, in this belief and mind of the Church, that Mary the mother of Jesus, the mother of this God-man, is the mother of God. What the Church proclaimed with the words "born of the virgin Mary," as having been handed down from the beginning by the apostles, was solemnly defined at the Council of Ephesus in 431, by the notion of the divine motherhood, which had already become a tradition. To this day Christians of all denominations are called upon to confess their belief in the divine motherhood of the blessed Virgin, with the whole of tradition, and the reformers of the sixteenth century too. There can indeed be no question of genuine Christianity, truly believing in the coming of God himself in human flesh, if this oldest of the articles of faith concerning Mary is no longer held firm, or if an attempt is made shamefacedly to disregard it. It is clear that only very little can be said here about this mystery of the faith, which really implies the whole substance of Christian belief. . . .

Thus Mary appears as a figure in sacred history, like Abraham and other characters in the historical dialogue between God and mankind, on whose right decision our salvation too depends, and on whom we are built up as on a foundation. We are told quite simply and plainly in Scripture: Look, there was a human being to whom an angel came with a mysterious message, and this human being said, simply and unreservedly: Be it done unto me according to thy word; and through these words of the blessed Virgin the Son of the eternal Father came down to this earth, to our flesh, into our history, and God has assumed for ever this world, in the flesh of his Son. And all that happened because Mary, by the consent of her faith, became the mother of God. The way Holy Scripture tells of her divine motherhood, then, involves Mary at once and as a matter of course in the tremendous, mysterious, shatteringly great drama that is being acted out between the eternal God and this world with its one human race. If, therefore, we wish to grasp or at least to form some idea of what is meant when the faith says she is the mother of God, the mother of the incarnate Word of the eternal Father, we must never view this motherhood as a merely physical one, but see it as a free, personal act of her faith, within the context of sacred history. We must also reflect, too, what we are really saying, when we confess with faith, as we genuflect, that *the Word was made flesh.* [Jn. 1, 14]

KARL RAHNER [121]

OCTOBER 15
ST. TERESA OF AVILA

Of mixed Christian and Jewish origins, Teresa Sánchez de Cepeda y Ahumada entered the rather relaxed and unhappy Carmelite Convent of Avila in 1534. After many years of indecisive religious commitment and serious illnesses, she was finally converted to a life of genuine prayer and with the help of some very great confessors—St. Francis Borgia, St. Peter of Alcantara, St. John of the Cross, among others!—resolutely embraced the call to perfection.

In later years, in cooperation with St. John of the Cross, she undertook the reform of the Carmelite Order and in particular, the founding of twenty-seven Carmelite monasteries for women. She also put into writing for the benefit of others her own experi-

ences with prayer and thereby became one of the great spiritual teachers of all time.

The value of mental prayer.

The blessings possessed by one who practises prayer—I mean mental prayer—have been written of by many saints and good men. Glory be to God for this! If it were not so, I should not have assurance enough (though I am not very humble) to dare to speak of it. I can say what I know by experience —namely, that no one who has begun this practice, however many sins he may commit, should ever forsake it. For it is the means by which we may amend our lives again, and without it amendment will be very much harder. So let him not be tempted by the devil, as I was, to give it up for reasons of humility, but let him believe that the words cannot fail of Him Who says that, if we truly repent and determine not to offend Him, He will resume His former friendship with us and grant us the favours which He granted aforetime, and sometimes many more, if our repentance merits it. And anyone who has not begun to pray, I beg, for love of the Lord, not to miss so great a blessing. There is no place here for fear, but only for desire. For, even if a person fails to make progress, or to strive after perfection, so that he may merit the consolations and favours given to the perfect by God, yet he will gradually gain a knowledge of the road to Heaven. And if he perseveres, I hope in the mercy of God, Whom no one has ever taken for a Friend without being rewarded; and mental prayer, in my view, is nothing but friendly intercourse, and frequent solitary converse, with Him Who we know loves us. If love is to be true and friendship lasting, certain conditions are necessary: on the Lord's side we know these cannot fail, but our nature is vicious, sensual and ungrateful. You cannot therefore succeed in loving Him as much as He loves you, because it is not in your nature to do so. If, then, you do not yet love Him, you will realize how much it means to you to have His friendship and how much He loves you, and you will gladly endure the troubles which arise from being so much with One Who is so different from you. . . .

I do not understand the fears of those who are afraid to begin

177

mental prayer: I do not know what they are afraid of. The devil does well to instil fear into us so that he may do us real harm. By making me afraid he stops me from thinking of the ways in which I have offended God and of all I owe Him and of the reality of hell and of glory and of the great trials and griefs which He suffered for me. That was the whole extent of my prayer, and remained so for as long as I was subject to these perils, and it was about these things that I used to think whenever I could; and very often, over a period of several years, I was more occupied in wishing my hour of prayer were over, and in listening whenever the clock struck, than in thinking of things that were good. Again and again I would rather have done any severe penance that might have been given me than practise recollection as a preliminary to prayer. It is a fact that, either through the intolerable power of the devil's assaults or because of my own bad habits, I did not at once betake myself to prayer; and whenever I entered the oratory I used to feel so depressed that I had to summon up all my courage to make myself pray at all. (People say that I have little courage, and it is clear that God has given me much more than to most women, only I have made bad use of it). In the end, the Lord would come to my help. Afterwards, when I had forced myself to pray, I would find that I had more tranquillity and happiness than at certain other times when I had prayed because I had wanted to. . . .

As I shall have a great deal to say about these consolations which the Lord gives to those who persevere in prayer, I am saying nothing here: I will only observe that prayer is the door to those great favours which He has bestowed upon me. Once the door is closed, I do not see how He will bestow them; for, though He may wish to take His delight in a soul and to give the soul delight, there is no way for Him to do so, since He must have it alone and pure, and desirous of receiving His favours. If we place numerous hindrances in His path, and do nothing to remove them, how can He come to us? And yet we wish God to grant us great favours!

ST. TERESA OF AVILA [122]

Of true friendships.

This Father [Baltasar Álvarez, her confessor from 1559 to 1564] began to lead me to greater perfection. He told me that I ought to leave nothing undone so as to become entirely pleasing to God, and he treated me with great skill, yet also very gently, for my soul was not at all strong, but very sensitive, especially as regards abandoning certain friendships which were not actually leading me to offend God. There was a great deal of affection beneath these and it seemed to me that if I abandoned them I should be sinning through ingratitude; so I asked him why it was necessary for me to be ungrateful if I was not offending God. He told me to commend the matter to God for a few days, and to recite the hymn *Veni, Creator,* and I should be enlightened as to which was the better thing to do. So I spent the greater part of one whole day in prayer; and then, beseeching the Lord that He would help me to please Him in everything, I began the hymn. While I was reciting it, there came to me a transport so sudden that it almost carried me away: I could make no mistake about this, so clear was it. This was the first time that the Lord had granted me the favour of any kind of rapture. I heard these words: "I will have thee converse now, not with men, but with angels." This simply amazed me, for my soul was greatly moved and the words were spoken to me in the depths of the spirit. For this reason they made me afraid, though on the other hand they brought me a great deal of comfort, which remained with me after the fear caused by the strangeness of the experience had vanished.

The words have come true: never since then have I been able to maintain firm friendship save with people who I believe love God and try to serve Him, nor have I derived comfort from any others or cherished any private affection for them. It has not been in my own power to do so; and it has made no difference if the people have been relatives or friends. Unless I know that a person loves God or practises prayer, it is a real cross to me to have to do with him. I really believe this is the absolute truth.

Since that day I have been courageous enough to give up everything for the sake of God, Who in that moment—for I think it happened in no more than a moment—was pleased to make

179

His servant another person. So there was need for my confessor to give me any further commands. When he had found me so much attached to these friendships, he had not ventured to tell me definitely to abandon them. He had to wait until the Lord took it in hand, as He did. I did not think at first that I could ever give them up, for I had tried it already, and it had caused me such great distress that I had put the idea aside, as the friendships did not appear unseemly. But now the Lord set me free and gave me strength to carry my resolution into practice. So I told my confessor this and gave up everything, exactly as he had instructed me to do. And when the persons with whom I had been intimate saw how determined I was it caused them great edification.

Blessed for ever be God, Who in one moment gave the freedom which, despite all the efforts I had been making for so many years, I had never been able to attain, though sometimes I had done such violence to myself that it badly affected my health. As it was the work of One Who is almighty and the true Lord of all, it caused me no distress.

ST. TERESA OF AVILA [123]

OCTOBER 18
ST. LUKE THE ENVANGELIST

The brother who is praised throughout all the churches. (Epistle)

That Paul preached to the Gentiles, and established churches from Jerusalem and around as far as Illyricum, is evident both from his own expressions, and from the testimony of Luke in the book of Acts. And in what provinces Peter also proclaimed the doctrine of Christ, the doctrine of the New Covenant, appears from his own writings, and may be seen from that epistle we have mentioned as admitted in the canon, and which he addressed to the Hebrews in the dispersion throughout Pontus, Galatia, Cappadocia, Asia, and Bithynia. But how many and which of these, actuated by a genuine zeal, were judged suitable to feed the churches established by these apostles, it is not easy to say, any

180

further than may be gathered from the writing of Paul. For he, indeed, had innumerable fellow labourers, or as he himself calls them, fellow soldiers in the church. Of these, the greater part are honoured with an indelible remembrance by him in his epistles, where he gives a lasting testimony concerning them. Luke also, in his Acts, speaking of his friends, mentions them by name. Timothy, indeed, is recorded as having first received the episcopate at Ephesus, as Titus also was appointed over the churches in Crete. But Luke, who was born at Antioch, and by profession a physician, being for the most part connected with Paul, and familiarly acquainted with the rest of the apostles, has left us two inspired books, the institutes of that spiritual healing art which he obtained from them. One of these is his Gospel, in which he testifies that he has recorded, *as those who were from the beginning eye-witnesses, and ministers of the word* [Lk. 1, 2], delivered to him, whom also, he says, he has in all things followed. The other is his Acts of the Apostles, which he composed, not from what he had heard from others, but from what he had seen himself. It is also said, that Paul usually referred to Luke's Gospel whenever in his epistles he spoke of some particular gospel of his own, saying, *according to my gospel.*

EUSEBIUS [124]

OCTOBER 28

STS. SIMON AND JUDE

If the world hates you, know that it has hated me before you. (Gospel)

It was inherent in the very nature of the world and the mission of Jesus, sent to raise reluctant human nature to the level of the divine, that a deadly endless conflict should exist between Him and the world. The world He regarded as His enemy, and its Prince, He said, is the devil. He did not even include the world in His prayer to his Father: *Not for the world do I pray.* [Jn. 17, 9] This conflict, and its culmination in the crucifixion, was so rooted in the nature of things as they are, that Simeon had predicted it at the Presentation: *Behold, this Child is destined for the fall and for the rise of many in Israel, and for a sign that shall be contradicted.* [Lk. 2, 34]

And as this conflict and contradiction was foreseen and predicted in the case of Jesus himself, so He in turn foretold that His disciples would be caught up in the same dread warfare with *the spirit of evil in the high places.* [Eph. 6, 12] They, too, were to drink of the chalice that He was to drink of; they were to be baptized with the baptism wherewith He was to be baptized. To them, therefore, He said: *If the world hates you, know that it has hated Me before you. If you were of the world, the world would love its own. But because you are not of the world, but I have chosen you out of the world, therefore the world hates you. Remember the word that I have spoken unto you: No servant is greater than His master. If they have persecuted Me, they will persecute you also.* [Jn. 15, 18–20]

These words, if specially applicable to the Apostles—and their successors—refer also to all Christians, as St. Paul in his turn affirms: *All who live godly in Christ Jesus shall suffer persecution.* [2 Tim. 3, 12] As to His Apostles, and those who share in their ministry, Jesus has these particular words: *They will expel you from the synagogues. Yes, the hour is coming for everyone who kills you to think that he is offering worship to God.* [Jn. 16, 2]

Wherever Jesus is truly presented and rightly known, no one will be indifferent to Him: they will either love Him or hate Him: whether in Himself or borne about by His Apostles. He is forever a sign of contradiction, set for the fall of some and for the rise of others, the object either of ardent love or furious hatred. So St. John describes it: *We are of God: He who knows God listens to us; he who is not of God does not listen to us. By this we know the spirit of truth and the spirit of error.* [1 Jn. 4, 5–6] Hence, the twofold, invariable mark of a truly supernatural apostolate is fruitfulness on the one and contradiction on the other. Wherever preaching does not produce this twofold result, it cannot be Jesus Christ Crucified Who is being preached. For Jesus Christ and His doctrine are a stumbling-block and foolishness, bringing all kinds of afflictions on His ministers: *For I think that God has set forth us the Apostles last of all, as men doomed to be spectacle to the*

world, and to angels, and to men. We are fools for Christ. . . .
We have become as the refuse of the world, the offscouring of all,
even till now! [4 Cor. 9–13]

Thus it may be stated *as a law* that governs supernatural activity in the ministry, as also the invariable pattern of divine activity shown in the works of all true disciples of Jesus, that they shall be signs of contradiction, wielding the two-edged sword of the word of God to reveal the thoughts of many hearts, that is, to find out at once the friends and the foes of Jesus. Says St. Alphonsus, affirming the existence of the law we speak of: "There is no remedy: for, says the Apostle, *All who live godly lives in Christ Jesus shall suffer persecution.* All who wish to follow Jesus Christ shall be persecuted. If, says St. Augustine, you are unwilling to suffer any persecution, tremble lest you have not as yet begun to serve Jesus Christ."

For those who are the ministers of the Word of God, St. Paul has stated this law in these words: *For we are the fragrance of Christ for God, alike as regards those who are saved and those who are lost: to these, an odor that leads to death; but to those, an odor that leads to life. . . . We, at least, are not, like many others, adulterating the word of God. . . . For we preach not ourselves, but Jesus Christ our Lord, and ourselves merely as your servant in Jesus.* [2 Cor. 2, 15–17; 4, 5]

If, then, persecution and contradiction suffered by priests in the course of their ministry is a scandal to certain Catholics, this is because they are living in ignorance of the nature of the Gospel message, the relation of this message to the world, and the *foreseen* effect of its impact upon the world. Who, indeed, were the men who rejected Christ's teaching and crucified Him? They were the Scribes and Pharisees: the leaders and teachers of the people: the men, divinely appointed, who sat in the chair of Moses and wielded his authority. Why was this? The Scriptures give the answer: the deadly, unending opposition between darkness and light: *The Light shines in the darkness, and the darkness grasped it not.* [Jn. 1, 15] Let us not be surprised at this opposition: for *what fellowship has light with darkness*? [2 Cor. 6, 14] None: hence the darkness could do nothing but seek to extinguish the Light of the world.

So it happened to Jesus. We take that fact for granted. That is our mistake—taking it for granted. So doing, we treat as only an historical fact, now long since past and gone, what was intended by God to be typical of what would happen to all who would follow Christ's teaching and example. Hence the persecution of the Church; hence also, *within* the Church, the persecution of the Saints by their fellow Catholics, and the similar persecution, also by fellow Catholics, of all who seriously try to conform their words or conduct to Christ's. Of course it is not the individuals as such who are persecuted: it is Christ Who is persecuted: it is the individual insofar as he reflects the Light. Hence the holiest men . . . are the most savagely persecuted.

JOHN J. HUGO [125]

CHRIST THE KING
(LAST SUNDAY OF OCTOBER)

That in all things he may hold the first place. (Epistle)

Christ is the Head not only of all mankind but of the whole physical universe; all things, in St. Paul's words, are to be gathered to a head in him. When he assumed a human nature, he assumed the whole universe in a certain sense into himself. For by the incarnation the whole universe is brought into organic relation with Christ and raised to a new mode of existence in him. When we assisted at mass we were assisting at the mystery of the "new creation," by which the whole world is destined to be transformed, passing from its present mode of extension in time and space into the eternal order of being in God. The creation was revealed for what it is, a symbol of the eternal reality manifested in time, a process of "becoming" always moving towards its realisation in the order of absolute being, where each creature will participate according to its capacity in the divine glory.

But still more intimately we were assisting at the return of mankind to its lost unity. Through the sacrifice of Christ mankind which had been divided by sin was restored to unity, and the sacrifice of the mass was the means by which this unity was being

184

achieved. Sin operates constantly as a force by which mankind is being divided, husband against wife, parents against children, class against class, and nation against nation. The sacrifice of Christ was the supreme power acting against this power of sin and drawing men into the unity of his Church.

BEDE GRIFFITHS [126]

What is the Redemption?
The re-establishment of the reign of God, which is the reign of love. It is by the establishment of the reign of God that the reign of self will be destroyed.

In whom was the reign of God first established?
In the Redeemer. Jesus was the perfect realization of the reign of God that he wants to establish in us. It was in him that human nature was first, so to speak, delivered from the human ego which had been its normal result, so that the divine Ego alone could animate it. The holy humanity of Christ is attached to the divine Personality in the subsistence of the Word, of the *Only Son who is in the bosom of the Father* [Jn. 1, 18]; and is aware of not belonging to itself; manifesting requirements which are eminently realized in it; able to demand everything because it demands nothing for itself; submissive in all it does to the movement of the Spirit; concerned only with the glory of God. This humanity is not a prison where Divinity will be held captive, but a Host from which it will radiate.

MAURICE ZUNDEL [127]

Thy kingdom come has also reference to that whereto *Thy will be done* refers—in us, that is. For when does God not reign, in whose hand is the heart of all kings? But whatever we wish for ourselves we augur for Him, and *to* Him we attribute what *from* Him we expect. And so, if the manifestation of the Lord's kingdom pertains unto the will of God and unto our anxious expectation, how do some pray for some protraction of the age, when the kingdom of God, which we pray may arrive, tends unto the consummation of the age? Our wish is, that our reign be hastened, not our servitude protracted. Even if it had not been prescribed in the Prayer that we should ask for the advent of the kingdom, we

185

should, unbidden, have sent forth that cry, hastening toward the realization of our hope. The souls of the martyrs beneath the altar cry in jealousy unto the Lord, *How long, Lord, dost Thou not avenge our blood on the inhabitants of the earth?* [Ap. 6, 10] for, of course, their avenging is regulated by the end of the age. Nay, Lord, Thy kingdom come with all speed, —the prayer of Christians, the confusion of the nations, the exultation of angels, for the sake of which we suffer, nay, rather, for the sake of which we pray!

TERTULLIAN [128]

The Kingdon of God is like a prince who went into a distant country to seek a crown for his return. [Lk. 19, 12] This little parable sums up the thought of early Christianity. Christ has been appointed a royal prince by his resurrection from the dead, and he is already seated upon his throne in heaven. But he is for the moment absent from his earthly kingdom, and we await his glorious return at any time.

The resurrection, the invisible, but very real and existing kingship of Christ, and the parousia, form the episodes in his reign.

The resurrection, in its positive aspect, the exaltation to the right hand of God, serves as the first enthronement of Christ, the real assumption of his office. Christ is in glory, he is seated on his heavenly throne. His enthronement is made known to the apostles who are the witnesses to his resurrection, and its effect is shown in the gifts of Pentecost.

The present kingdom of Christ is, however, only an intermediate stage. The spiritual effects are manifested, but nothing is accomplished. The charisms are only portents of the rewards to be received in time to come. The subjects of the kingdom are ennobled, glorified, raised up only in an invisible manner, for it is the kingdom of the resurrection of the dead, of the world to come. The material world always yearns for the final manifestation, but the king himself is now invisible, and his apparitions are only intermittent and by way of preparation, and his interventions are limited to the governing of the Church.

Then the great event will occur for which the world has hoped for so long, and towards which everything is directed. Christ will

186

reveal his glory and his power on the great day, he will destroy the hostile Powers, and then he will restore the kingdom to his Father.

The connections between the intermediate and definitive periods are made clear in various ways.

Our idea of imperfection is too much mixed up with the theory of evolution and development to represent the thought of Saint Paul. The present world is not raised up little by little to the definitive kingdom of Christ, but it remains always in an inferior and worldly state in relation to it, and creation "sighs for" the appearance of God's glory. If there is any belief, this belief is also of an inferior order, for it is a quantitative, not a qualitative belief, with the result that the establishing of the eschatological kingdom will always be an event of another order. This will be the harvest gathered by the angels of God, with the tree passing suddenly from the sapling stage to full maturity so that birds of heaven may build their nests in its branches.

The relationship between the two is really that between an image and reality, between a "mystery" and that which is clear. It is to these formulas that we must confine ourselves if we wish to follow the advance of early Christian thought.

Then again, the world to come and its image belong to the same higher order by the fact that they are both opposed to the present "world." In fact, the same reality is found either in all clarity or in the mystery. There are always two gaps to consider at one and the same time: the gaps between the fleshly and spiritual realities, and between the state of the spiritual as mystery and of the spiritual that has become visible. The passing from mystery to clarity involves a complete reversal, with the divine, invisible world becoming perceptible and imposing itself on angels and men, while the material and fleshly world appears in all its emptiness.

The first gap is filled in for Christians, for the knowledge of spiritual truths has been granted to us. We know God, we know what rewards and graces await us in heaven. We have the Spirit, and the riches of the kingdom of God. We are made one with Christ, and we have already risen again. But the second gap remains, and the progress which we make in our present stage does not bring us any nearer to the other stage, so that there is still the profound difference between the mystery and its shining manifestation.

LUCIEN CERFAUX [129]

I am a King! (Gospel)

Men have imagined that the acknowledgment of the divinity of Christ relieves them of the obligation of taking His words seriously. They have twisted certain texts of the Gospel so as to get out of them the meaning they want, while they have conspired to pass over in silence other texts which do not lend themselves to such treatment. The precept *Render to Caesar the things that are Caesar's, and to God the things that are God's* [Mt. 22, 21] is constantly quoted to sanction an order of things which gives Caesar all and God nothing. The saying *My Kingdom is not of this world* [Jn. 18, 36] is always being used to justify and confirm the paganism of our social and political life, as though Christian society were destined to belong to this world and not to the Kingdom of Christ. On the other hand the saying *All power is given Me in heaven and* earth [Mt. 28, 18] is never quoted. Men are ready to accept Christ as sacrificing Priest and atoning Victim; but they do not want Christ the King. His royal dignity has been ousted by every kind of pagan despotism, and Christian peoples have taken up the cry of the Jewish rabble: *We have no king but Caesar!* [Jn. 19, 15] Thus history has witnessed, and we are still witnessing, the curious phenomenon of a society which professes Christianity as its religion but remains pagan not merely in its life but in the very basis of that life.

This dichotomy is not so much a logical *non sequitur* as a moral failure. That is obvious from the hypocrisy and sophism which are characteristic of the arguments commonly used to justify this state of affairs. "Slavery and severe hardship," said a bishop renowned in Russia thirty years ago, "are not contrary to the spirit of Christianity; for physical suffering is not a hindrance to the salvation of the soul, which is the one and only end of our religion." As though the infliction of physical suffering by a man on his fellow-men did not imply in him a moral depravity and an

188

act of injustice and cruelty which were certainly imperilling the salvation of his soul! Granted even—though the supposition is absurd—that a Christian society can be insensible to the sufferings of the oppressed, the question remains whether it can be indifferent to the sins of the oppressors.

Economic slavery, even more than slavery properly so called, has found its champions in the Christian world. Society and the State, they maintain, are in no way bound to take general and regular measures against pauperism; voluntary almsgiving is enough; did not Christ say that there would always be the poor on earth? Yes, there will always be the poor; there will also always be the sick, but does that prove the uselessness of health services? Poverty in itself is no more an evil than sickness; the evil consists in remaining indifferent to the sufferings of one's neighbor. And it is not a question only of the poor; the rich also have a claim on our compassion. These poor rich! We do everything to develop their bump of acquisitiveness, and then we expect them to enter the Kingdom of God through the imperceptible opening of individual charity. Besides, it is well known that authoritative scholars see in the phrase 'the eye of a needle' simply a literal translation of the Hebrew name given to one of the gates of Jerusalem (*negeb-ha-khammath* or *khur-ha-khammath*) which it was difficult for camels to pass through. Surely then it is not the infinitesimal contribution of personal philanthropy which the Gospel enjoins upon the rich, but rather the narrow and difficult, but nevertheless practicable, way of social reform.

VLADIMIR SOLOVYEV [130]

Nothing will serve better to promote an appreciation of these blessings and to spread them far and wide through society than the institution of a special feast in honor of the Kingship of Christ. For people are taught the truths of the faith and brought to appreciate them more effectively by the annual celebration of the sacred mysteries than by official pronouncements of the Church. For such pronouncements usually reach only the few and, for the most part, the learned; feasts reach *all* the Faithful. Pronouncements speak once; feasts speak every year, in fact forever. The Church's teaching impresses the mind primarily, while her feasts influence both mind and heart, affecting the whole of man's nature. For man is made up of body and soul and needs these external functions. These sacred rites in all their varied beauty stimulate man to a deeper penetration of the truths God has revealed. Thus they become part of his very life.

PIUS XI [131]

November

All Saints
All Souls
St. Martin de Porres
The Dedication of Churches
St. Martin of Tours
St. John of the Cross
St. Andrew

ALL SAINTS

In the earthly liturgy we take part in a foretaste of that heavenly liturgy which is celebrated in the holy city of Jerusalem towards which we journey as pilgrims, where Christ is sitting at the right hand of God, a minister of the holies and of the true tabernacle; we sing a hymn to the Lord's glory with all the warriors of the heavenly army; venerating the memory of the saints, we hope for some part and fellowship with them; we eagerly await the Savior, our Lord Jesus Christ, until he, our life, shall appear and we too will appear with him in glory.

CONSTITUTION ON THE SACRED LITURGY [132]

To the heights.

I have this day climbed the highest mountain in this district—its name of Ventosus is not undeserved—guided only by a desire to behold what one could see from so extraordinary a height. The thought of such an expedition had been with me for many years. For, as you are aware, I have, by decree of the fate which governs the affairs of men, dwelt in these parts; and the mountain, visible from every point of vantage, is almost constantly before my eyes. At length an impulse seized me finally to put into action what I was daily doing in thought; and then also I happened to be reading yesterday Livy's history of Rome, and by chance my eye lighted on the passage which tells how Philip, King of Macedon (he who fought a war with the Roman people), ascended Mount Haemus in Thessaly.

But when I bethought myself of a suitable companion, scarcely any of my friends, strangely enough, seemed satisfactory in every respect. One seemed too inactive, another too easy-going; one too slow, and another too fast; one too sad, and another too cheerful. This one was more prudent than I could wish, and that one too rash. The silence of the one, the forwardness of another, this one's gravity and stoutness, that one's effervescence and leanness, deterred me. I was discouraged by the cool indifference of the one and the ardent enthusiasm of another. . . . At last I turned homeward for help, and related the affair to my only brother, who is younger than I and well known to you. He listened with the greatest pleasure, being delighted at my considering him a friend as well as a brother.

On the appointed day we set out from home and arrived by evening at Malaucene, a place at the foot of the mountain, looking north. After staying there a day, we finally climbed the mountain today, with a servant apiece and not without difficulty, since it proved to be an almost inaccessibly steep mass of earth. But *labor omnia vincit improbus,* as the poet well says. The long day, the mild air, the strength and agility of our bodies, and everything else of the same sort aided us on. Our only obstacle was the terrain itself. We met an old shepherd in a valley below the mountain, who tried with many words to dissuade us from the climb. He himself (he said) had once climbed to the very top on an impulse of youthful enthusiasm, and had brought back nothing for his pains save pain and effort. His body and his clothes had been torn by the stones and briars. Never, before or since, had there been any talk of anyone's doing as much. While he was shouting these things at us, our desire only grew with each of his warnings—the minds of young people are always incredulous of those who admonish them. Accordingly, when the old man saw that his endeavor were of no avail, he went ahead of us a little way and pointed with his finger to a steep path between the rocks, at the same time giving us a good deal of advice. This last he kept on repeating after we had left him. Having placed in his care whatever of our clothes and other possessions might prove an impediment, we dedicated ourselves vigorously to the ascent and mounted quickly with no other companions.

But, as usually happens, we had no sooner harnessed our energies than we suddenly grew weary. Having gone ahead a little way to the top of a cliff, we were compelled to halt. Then we started anew and pushed forward, though at a much slower pace. My brother, taking a path straight up the mountain, was making for the top; but I, less energetic, was turning downwards, and when called back by my brother and shown the right road I answered that I hoped to find the ascent easier on the other side and would not mind going a greater distance if only I could proceed with less difficulty. Thus I excused my own laziness; and meanwhile my brother was already quite a distance up the mountain, though I was meandering about in the valleys below, by no means finding an easier road and as a matter of fact growing weary by reason of my useless efforts. Then, exhausted and disgusted with myself for walking about aimlessly, I finally resolved to seek the heights and at length, tired and out of breath, joined my brother, who was waiting for me and was quite refreshed as a result. For a time we walked on, side by side. But ere long, forgetting what had happened before, I was straying downward again.

Then, my thoughts flitting suddenly from material to incorporeal things, I addressed these words (or others like them) to myself: "What you have experienced today quite frequently while climbing this mountain, you cannot help knowing is like what happens to you and to many who enter into a life of blessedness; for the life which we term 'blessed' also lies in a high place. Narrow is the way which leads unto it, we are told. Many also are the hills which bar the way, and we must climb with mighty steps from virtue to virtue." I cannot tell you how elevating this thought was to my mind, and my body also seemed spurred on to make what remained of the ascent. . . .

At the top is a little level space on which we rested at last after so much effort. At first, deeply moved by a quality in the air to which I was unaccustomed and by the unrestricted view, I was like one stupified. I looked down; the clouds were under my feet. And now Athos and Olympus were become less incredible to me, beholding as I did in a mountain of lesser fame what I had heard and read of them. Then I turned my eyes towards Italy, which is dearest to my heart. The Alps themselves, stiff and snowclad, through which the fierce enemy of the Roman name once crossed breaking (if we credit the story) the rocks with vinegar, seemed so close to me even though they really were far away. I shall confess that I sighed for the skies of Italy, visible to my mind rather than to my eyes; and a boundless longing came upon me to see my friends and my native land again.

Then a different thought engrossed my mind, diverting it from places to time. I said to myself, "Today it is ten years since you left Bologna, having abandoned the studies of your boyhood. O immortal God! O immutable Wisdom! How many changes, and

194

what great ones, in your character has the time which has passed since then witnessed. I pass over countless things, for I am not yet so safe in port that I can calmly recall the storms through which I passed. Perhaps the time will come when I shall run through them all in the order of their occurrence, prefacing them with the words of your Augustine, 'I desire to recall my past foulness and the carnal corruptions of my soul, not because I love them, but because I would love you, O my God!' "

PETRARCH [133]

All the treasures of the saints are at our disposal.

We do not dispose solely our strength for loving, understanding and serving God, but of everything at once, from the Blessed Virgin at the summit of all the heavens to that poor African leper who, a bell in his hand, uses a mouth half rotted away to breathe out the responses of the mass. All creation visible and invisible, all history, all the past, all the present and all the future, all nature, all the treasure of the saints multiplied by Grace—all that is at our disposal, all that is our prolongation and our prodigious equipment. All the saints and all the angels are ours. We can use the intelligence of Saint Thomas, the arm of Saint Michael, the heart of Joan of Arc and of Catherine of Siena. We have only to touch all the latent resources in us to see them rise up. All that is good and important and beautiful from one end of the earth to the other, all that creates holiness in the world, is, in a sense, our work. We participate in the heroism of missionaries, in the inspiration of doctors, in the generosity of martyrs, in the genius of artists, in the burning prayer of the nuns of St. Clare and the Carmelites. From the north to the south, from alpha to omega, from the east to the west, all is one with us, we are clothed with it, we instigate it, we are both revealed and humbled in this orchestral operation . . . in the immense encompassing of Christianity.

PAUL CLAUDEL [134]

Behold the lively example of the holy fathers and blessed saints in whom flourished and shone all true perfection of life and all perfect religion, and you will see how little, almost nothing, we do nowadays in comparison with them.

Oh, what is our life when it is compared to theirs? They served our Lord in hunger and in thirst, in fear, in cold, in nakedness, in labor and in weariness, in vigils and fastings, in prayer and in holy meditations, in persecutions and in many reproofs.

Oh, how many and how grievous tribulations the apostles, martyrs, confessors, virgins, and other holy saints suffered who were willing to follow the steps of Christ. They refused honors and all bodily pleasures here in this life that they might have everlasting life. Oh, how strict and how abject a life the holy fathers in the wilderness led. How grievous the temptations they suffered, and how fiercely they were assailed by their spiritual enemies. How fervent the prayer they daily offered to God, what rigorous abstinence they kept. What great zeal and fervor they had for spiritual profit, how strong a battle they waged against all sin, and how pure and entire their purpose toward God in all their deeds!

In the day they labored and in the night they prayed, and though they labored bodily in the day, they prayed in mind, and so they always spent their time fruitfully. They felt every hour short for the service of God, and because of the great sweetness they had in heavenly contemplation they often forgot their bodily nourishment. All riches, honor, dignity, kinsmen, and friends they renounced for the love of God. They desired to have nothing in the world, and scarcely would they take what was necessary for their bodily sustenance.

They were poor in worldly goods, but they were rich in grace and virtue; they were needy outwardly, but inwardly in their souls they were replenished with grace and spiritual comfort. To the world they were aliens and strangers, but to God they were dear and familiar friends. In the sight of the world and in their own sight they were vile and mean, but in the sight of God and of His saints they were precious and singularly elect. In them shone forth all perfection of virtue—true meekness, simple obedience, charity and patience, with other similar virtues and gracious gifts of God; and so, they profited daily in spirit and obtained great grace from God. They are left as an example to all religious persons, and their lives should stir us to devotion, and to advance more and more in virtue and grace, than should the example of dissolute and idle persons hinder us in any way.

THOMAS A KEMPIS [135]

NOVEMBER 2
ALL SOULS

The Church Suffering and the Church Militant constitute in their relations a second circle of most vital activities. Having entered into the night "wherein no man can work," the Suffering Church cannot ripen to its final blessedness by any efforts of its own, but only through the help of others—through the intercessory prayers and sacrifices (*suffragia*) of those living members of the Body of Christ who being still in this world are able in the grace of Christ to perform expiatory works. The Church has from the earliest times faithfully guarded the words of Scripture that *it is a holy and a wholesome thing to pray for the dead that they may be loosed from their sins.* [2 Macc. 12, 43] The suppliant cry of her liturgy: "Eternal rest give to them, O Lord, and let perpetual light shine upon them," can be heard already in the Acts of the martyrdom of SS. Perpetua and Felicitas (A.D. 203) and is represented in numerous sepulchral inscriptions of the most ancient period, while theologians and Fathers of the Church, beginning with Tertullian, have supplied its substantial proof. . . . So fundamental indeed and so natural to man's hope and desire and love is this belief, that historians of religion have discovered it among almost all non-Christian civilised peoples: a striking illustration of Tertullian's saying that the human soul is naturally Christian.

The Catholic, therefore, is jealous to expiate and suffer for the "poor souls," especially by offering the Eucharistic Sacrifice, wherein Christ's infinite expiation on the Cross is sacramentally re-presented, and stimulating and joining itself with the expiatory

197

works of the faithful, passes to the Church Suffering according to the measure determined by God's wisdom and mercy. So the saying of St. Paul that the members of the Body of Christ *are mutually careful one for another* [1 Cor. 12, 25] is nowhere more comprehensively and luminously fulfilled than in the Church's suffrages for her dead children. When, in the Memento of the Mass, in the presence of the sacred Oblation and under the gaze so to speak of the Church Triumphant, she cries to heaven: "Be mindful also, O Lord, of thy servants and handmaids. . . . who have gone before us with the sign of faith and rest in the sleep of peace," then truly heaven and earth greet each other, the Church Triumphant, Suffering and Militant meet in a "holy kiss," and the "whole" Christ with all His members celebrates a blessed love-feast (*agapē*), a memorial of their communion in love and joy and pain.

KARL ADAM [136]

A warning to those who mourn excessively.

"What, then," you will ask, "is a man not allowed to weep, though he is human?"

I do not forbid this, but I do forbid tearing yourself to pieces; I do forbid weeping without restraint. I am not brutal or cruel; I know that human nature is tried [by the death of dear ones] and misses their companionship and daily converse with them. It is impossible not to show grief. Christ also showed it, for He wept because of Lazarus. Follow His example yourself: weep, but gently, with decorum, with the fear of God. If you weep in this way, you do so, not as if you were without faith in the resurrection, but as one finding the separation hard to bear.

Besides, we also weep for those who are going away from home, or who are going on a journey, but we do not do this as if we were in despair. Weep in this way, then, at the death of a dear one, as if you were bidding farewell to one setting out on a journey. I am telling you this, not as an impersonal rule of conduct, but in consideration of your human nature. For, if the dead man is a sinner who has committed many offenses against God, you ought to weep, or, rather, not only to weep (for that is no help to him), but you ought to do what can give him assistance, namely, give alms and offer sacrifices. Furthermore, you ought to rejoice for this advantage, namely, that the opportunity to do evil deeds has been taken away from him.

On the contrary, if he was a just man, you ought to be still happier, because his fate now rests secure and he is free from uncertainty for the time to come. If he is a young man, you ought to be happy because he has been quickly freed from the evils of this life; if he is old, because he has departed this life after having received in its fullness what seems to be desirable. . . . Truly, honor for the dead does not consist in lamentations and moanings, but in singing hymns and psalms and living a noble life. For the man who has departed this life will go on his way in the company of the angels, even if no one is present at his funeral; while he who has been corrupt will gain no profit, even if he has the entire city sending him off to the grave.

Do you wish to honor the departed? Honor him in other ways; namely, by giving alms, performing good works, taking part in the divine services. What good is done him by copious weeping? . . .

Let us look heavenward; let us reflect on spiritual considerations. How shall we be able to refute the heathen? How shall we be able to exhort them if we do such things? How shall we preach to them of the resurrection? How shall we discuss with them the rest of the Christian doctrines? How shall we ourselves live in security? Do you not know that death may be caused by grief? Darkening the soul's spiritual vision not only prevents it from perceiving what it should, but even causes it much harm. By showing excessive grief, therefore, we offend God and help neither ourselves nor the departed.

By restraining our grief, on the contrary, we both please God and conduct ourselves becomingly in the eyes of men. For, if we ourselves do not succumb unrestrainedly to grief, He will quickly take away the portion of grief we feel; whereas, if we give way to excessive grief, He will permit us to become entirely possessed by it. If we give thanks for it, we shall not be disheartened.

"Yet how is it possible for a man not to grieve," you will ask, "when he has lost his son, or his daughter, or his wife?"

I am not saying: "Do not grieve," but: "Do not give way to

unrestrained grief." For, if we reflect that it is God who has taken him away, that it was a mortal husband or son we had, we shall quickly feel consoled. Excessive grief indicates that those who give way to it are seeking for something that is above and beyond nature. You were born a man, and therefore mortal; why, then, do you repine because something has happened in accordance with nature? You do not repine, do you, because you are nourished by eating food? You do not seek to maintain your life without this, do you? Act thus, also, in regard to death, and do not try to obtain immortality in the present life, though you are but mortal.

This doctrine has now been once and for all defined. Do not give way to excessive grief, do not tear yourself to pieces, but be resigned to the lot decreed for us all in common. Grieve, rather, for your sins. This is in truth the best kind of sorrow; this is the soundest practice of Christian teachings.

ST. JOHN CHRYSOSTOM [137]

NOVEMBER 3
ST. MARTIN DE PORRES

Martin (1579–1639) was born in Lima, Peru, of mixed parentage, his father a Spaniard, his mother a Negro. A Dominican lay brother for forty-five years, he was famed for his corporal and spiritual works of mercy and for his Francis of Assisi-like power over birds and animals. He has become the unofficial patron of the American movement for interracial justice.

The real question that is raised by non-violent action is not at all whether the democratic ideal ought to be replaced by something else: it is on the contrary an accusation of those who, while mouthing democratic slogans, have in fact clearly betrayed the democratic ideal and emptied it of meaning. This explains the virulence of the counterattack against the kind of thinking which non-violence supposes.

Non-violence does not attack the ideals on which democratic society is built, still less the ideals of Christianity. It claims instead to be a genuine fulfillment and implementation of those ideals. In so claiming, moreover, it rejects the counter-claim of that popular self-understanding which is in fact a secular myth and a betrayal of democracy and of Christianity.

The real question which non-violent action poses is this: whether it may not in fact be necessary to practice non-violent methods if democracy is to be kept alive and preserved against the sclerosis which is gradually hardening it into a new form of Totalism.

If, instead of fabricating for ourselves a mythical and inadequate self-understanding made up of the postures and antics of TV westerns, we return to a deeper awareness of our professed ideals, we may find that non-violence is very relevant to them. After all, the basic principle of non-violence is respect for the personal conscience of the opponent. Non-violent action is a way of insisting on one's just rights without violating the rights of anyone else. In many instances, non-violence offers the only possible way in which this can be effected. The whole strength of non-violence depends on this absolute respect for the rights even of an otherwise unjust oppressor: his legal rights and his moral rights as a person. If non-violence is allied with civil disobedience, and it certainly is, this disobedience is, however, strictly limited. It is confined to *disobeying an unjust law,* for only this disobedience can be carried out without violation of rights.

Where an unjust law is disobeyed, non-violent resistance nevertheless supposes *implicit acceptance of the penalty* which is imposed for violation of the law. The purpose of this disobedience and the prompt acceptance of punishment for it is, according to Gandhian principles, to make abundantly clear the injustice of the law, in such a way that even the unjust oppressor will come to admit the fact, and will himself be willing to help change the situation.

In this way, non-violence claims to work not only for the good of the one who is unjustly oppressed, but also for the good of the oppressor. Ideally speaking, non-violent action is supposed to be conducted in such a way that both sides come to see the injustice as a disadvantage and a dishonor to both, and they then agree to work together to remedy things. In this way, non-violence aims not at disruption and disintegration of society, but at a more real and living collaboration, based on truth and love.

So much for the ideal.

It must certainly be admitted that not all those who claim to be practicing non-violence have kept themselves strictly within the limits so prescribed. On the contrary, many have in fact a very imperfect understanding of these principles and have made their non-violence simply another form of violence. But on the other hand, those who have taken non-violence seriously enough to dedicate their lives to it, have undergone the necessary training, and have carried out their tasks with the required discipline, have not only achieved great success but have demonstrated the truth of the principles. In spite of all attempts at misrepresentation and denigration, these achievements have been evident and impressive. The witness of genuine non-violence has been incontestable.

It is unfortunate that, along with dedicated and disciplined non-violence there has been much irresponsibility and even immoral and anti-social protest which the general public has not easily distinguished from the real thing.

The mass media have been content to keep this distinction blurred and the whole concept of non-violence remains, as far as most Americans are concerned, on the level of fearsome and repugnant myth.

We badly need a clear, sound, fundamental treatment of the principles of non-violent action. The chief value of such an exposition is first of all that it will distinguish between non-violence and non-resistance. Not only does non-violence resist evil, but, if it is properly practiced, it resists evil more effectively than violence ever could. Indeed, the chief argument in favor of non-violent resistance is that it is, *per se* and ideally, *the only really effective resistance to injustice and evil.*

This does not mean that in practice the solution to grave international and civil problems can be had merely by good will and pious gestures of appeasement. The non-violent ideal does not contain in itself all the answers to all our questions. These will have to be met and worked out amid the risks and anguish of day-to-day politics. But they can never be worked out if non-violence is never taken seriously.

In any event, the reader may rest assured that if, on putting down this essay, he feels himself "inclined to non-violence," he does not have to fear that his mind will presently snap and that he will go berserk. At least one thing should be clear by now. Far from being a fanatical manifestation of misguided idealism, non-violence demands a lucid reason, a profound religious faith, and above all, an uncompromising and courageous spirit of self-sacrifice.

THOMAS MERTON [138]

NOVEMBER 9
THE DEDICATION OF THE BASILICA OF THE HOLY SAVIOUR

(St. John Lateran)

This dedication feast (and that of November 18) recalls the purpose and sanctity of Christian churches where God's word is proclaimed and the mysteries duly celebrated. It also reminds us of the world-wide Catholic Church of which each local congregation and edifice is an image, and of the heavenly City, the goal of our pilgrimage.

The Church is the building of God.

Often the Church has been called the *building* of God. [1 Cor. 3, 9] The Lord himself compared himself to the stone which the builders rejected, but which was made into the cornerstone. [Mt. 21, 42, etc.] On this foundation the Church is built by the apostles [see 1 Cor. 3, 11], and from it the Church receives solidity and cohesion. This edifice has many names to describe it: the house of God, in which his *family* dwells; the dwelling of God in the Spirit (Eph. 2, 19, 22); the tabernacle of God among men (Ap. 21, 3); and, especially, the holy *temple*. This *temple*, symbolized in sanctuaries of stone, is praised by the holy Fathers and, not without reason, is compared in the liturgy to the holy city, the new Jerusalem. As living stones, we here on earth are built into it. [1 Pet. 2, 5]

CONSTITUTION ON THE CHURCH [139]

Today salvation has come to this house. (Gospel)

The Church is the visible shape of salvation, the sign filled with the reality it signifies. Its members can therefore sin only to the extent to which they positively withdraw themselves from its sanctifying influence. To the extent that a man sins, he is outside the Church; in himself, and thus in his place in the Church, he brings about a rupture between the sign and the reality it signifies. All of this implies that the Church has not yet reached its final state. For we cannot hold that it will cease to exist at the end of time, and make place for a purely spiritual communion of the saints in grace. In virtue of Christ's incarnation the bodily visibility of grace is not a provisional and temporary measure but the definitive reality. Only in heaven will the Church reach its full maturity, still as a visible saving society. The resurrection of all flesh establishes and perpetuates in glory the earthly history of the Church, just as the personal holiness which the saints have fought for and won in this life will be visible in their bodies when they rise again. All that is weak and sad and troublesome will have disappeared from the Church in heaven, but it will continue to show us the face of its holiness in the visibility that comes of incarnation. Indeed, only in heaven shall we see this to the full.

The Church, as the earthly sign of the triumph of Christ's grace, still remains in a state of weakness, needing to purge itself of all that is sinful. This fact shows us two things; first that the glory of the Church on earth is a veiled glory, for around it there is still a broad margin of weakness and shortcoming; and second, and more especially, that the power of God is fulfilled in and through the weakness and poverty of the Church. The Church is great and glorious, but not on account of its earthly strength and achievements; in it Christ's redeeming grace always triumphs in spite of human weakness. It is in this weakness that the divine power comes into its own and becomes visible as divine. The Church is therefore not only the object of our faith; it is also the test of our faith. It can become an obstacle and a danger to faith. For belief is not a conviction to which a person is forced by the glory of the Church manifest in his experience of her. We always believe in the midst of darkness. And if we look at it in this way, the weakness of the Church is a *felix culpa,* for it makes us realize that our only boast is in the power of God. Just as Christ was a scandal to the Jews because to the Jewish mind he set himself up in opposition to Yahweh, so too the Church must pass through its pilgrimage, poor and despised, for the power of redeeming grace alone will bring the victory. This is the real strength of our faith in the Church.

EDWARD SCHILLEBEECKX [140]

NOVEMBER 11
ST. MARTIN OF TOURS

A native of the Roman province of Pannonia (roughly modern day Hungary), Martin spontaneously became a catechumen at the age of ten and was drafted into the Roman army in his teens. After securing his release from military service he first experimented with the eremetical life in Italy and then became a disciple of St. Hilary of Poitiers. As such he was one of the outstanding propagators of primitive monasticism in Gaul, a zealous opponent of the Arian heresy, a rather rigid and uncompromising bishop even in the face of tyrannical political power, and the great apostle of the still pagan countryside. Renowned for his miracles, his charity, and his spiritual direction, he died in 397 and became the first confessor bishop to have a liturgical feast in the Western Church. In the middle ages his glorious tomb at Tours was the goal of great pilgrimages and his cape the palladium of the French royal house.

So it came about that one day when he had nothing on him but his weapons and his uniform, in the middle of a winter which had been fearfully hard beyond the ordinary, so that many were dying of the intense cold, he met at the city gate of Amiens a coatless beggar. This beggar had been asking the passers-by to take pity on him but all had gone past the unfortunate creature. Then the God-filled man understood, from the fact that no one else had had pity, that this beggar had been reserved for him. But what was he to do? He had nothing with him but the cape he had on, for he had already used up what else he had, in similar good works. So

205

he took the sword he was wearing and cut the cape in two and gave one half to the beggar, putting on the rest himself again.

This raised a laugh from some of the bystanders, for he looked grotesque in the mutilated garment; but many had more sense, and sighed to think that they had not done something of the kind; indeed, having more to give, they could have clothed the beggar without stripping themselves. And that night, in his sleep, Martin saw Christ wearing the half of his cape with which he had clothed the beggar. He was told to look carefully at Our Lord and take note that it was the garment that he had given away. Then he heard Jesus say aloud to the throng of angels that surrounded Him: "Martin is still only a catechumen 'but he has clothed Me with this garment."

SEVERUS [141]

After his baptism Martin sought release from the army.

Meanwhile the barbarians were making incursions into Gaul and the Caesar Julian concentrated his army at Worms. There he began to distribute a bonus to the soldiers. They were called up one by one in the usual way until Martin's turn came. But he thought it would be a suitable time for applying for his discharge, for he did not think that it would be honest for him to take the bonus if he was not going to fight. So he said to the Caesar: "I have been your soldier up to now. Let me now be God's. Let someone who is going to fight have your bonus. I am Christ's soldier; I am not allowed to fight."

These words put the tyrant in a rage and he said that it was from fear of the battle that was to be fought the next day that he wanted to quit the service, not from religious motives. But Martin was undaunted; in fact he stood all the firmer when they tried to frighten him.

"If it is put down to cowardice," he said, "and not to faith, I will stand unarmed in front of the battle-line tomorrow and I will go unscathed through the enemy's columns in the name of the Lord Jesus, protected by the sign of the Cross instead of by shield and helmet."

So he was ordered to be removed into custody so that he could

206

prove his words and face the barbarians unarmed. The next day the enemy sent envoys to ask for peace, surrendering themselves and all they had. Who can doubt in these circumstances that this victory was due to this man of blessings and was granted to him so that he should not be sent unarmed into the battle? The good Lord could have kept His soldier safe even among the swords and javelins of the enemy but, to spare those hallowed eyes the sight of other men's deaths, He made a battle unnecessary. For Christ could not rightly have granted any other victory for the benefit of His own soldier than one in which the enemy were beaten bloodlessly and no man had to die.

SEVERUS [142]

As a bishop, Martin preserved his virtue in the face of imperial blandishments.

Many bishops from various parts of the world had assembled to meet the Emperor Maximus, a man ferocious by nature and, moreover, elated by his victory in a civil war. The foul fawning of all of them upon the sovereign was much remarked, and the dignity of the priesthood with unworthy weakness lowered itself to win imperial patronage. Martin alone retained Apostolic authority. For even when he had to petition the Emperor on somebody's behalf, he commanded rather than requested and, though frequently invited to his banquets, he [normally] kept away. . . .

Invitations were sent out as if for a great festival and among the guests were men of the very highest rank, including Evodius, who was Prefect, and Consul also, and one of the most upright men that ever lived, and two Counts wielding immense authority, the brother and the uncle of the Emperor. Between these sat one of Martin's priests, Martin himself occupying a stool placed next to the Emperor. Towards the middle of the meal a servant, in accordance with custom, brought a goblet to the Emperor. He ordered it to be given instead to our most holy Bishop and waited expectantly to receive it from the Bishop's own hands. But Martin, after drinking himself, passed the goblet to his priest, holding that no one had a better right to drink immediately after himself and that it would not be honest of him to give precedence over

207

the priest either to the Emperor or to those who ranked next to him.

The Emperor and all who were present were so struck by this action that the very gesture by which they had been humiliated became for them a source of pleasure. And the news went all round the palace that Martin had done at the Emperor's table what no other bishop would have done even when dining with the least of his magistrates.

SEVERUS [143]

NOVEMBER 24
ST. JOHN OF THE CROSS

John de Yepes was born at Fontiveros near Avila in 1542, studied under the Jesuits in his teens, and became a Carmelite friar in 1563. In the same year that he was ordained to the priesthood (1567), he met St. Teresa of Avila and was persuaded to join her Discalced Reform. Although he was ultimately successful in founding several reform houses and in getting them erected into a separate province in 1580, ten years later he was deposed from all his offices and died in exile a year later.

Like his life the doctrine of John of the Cross urges the absolute necessity of detachment. As a great master of the spiritual life his mystical writings center upon the necessity of purifying the soul of all that is not divine so that God may use it as a perfectly docile instrument of his will.

Persons who want to attain to divine unions must be free of all desires, however slight they be.

Voluntary desires, whether they be of mortal sin, which are the gravest, or of venial sin, which are less grave, or whether they be only of imperfections, which are the least grave of all, must be driven away every one, and the soul must be free from them all, howsoever slight they be, if it is to come to this complete union; and the reason is that the state of this Divine union consists in the soul's total transformation, according to the will, in the will of

God, so that there may be naught in the soul that is contrary to the will of God, but that, in all and through all, its movement may be that of the will of God alone. . . .

Upon this road we must ever journey in order to attain our goal; which means that we must ever be mortifying our desires and not indulging them; and if they are not all completely mortified we shall not completely attain. For even as a log of wood may fail to be transformed in the fire because a single degree of heat is wanting to it, even so the soul will not be transformed in God if it have but one imperfection, although it be something less than voluntary desire; for, as we shall say hereafter concerning the night of faith, the soul has only one will, and that will, if it be embarrassed by aught and set upon aught, is not free, solitary and pure, as is necessary for Divine transformation.

ST. JOHN OF THE CROSS [144]

After warning of the dangers of unmortified desires, John provides a few brief counsels for conquering voluntary desires.

First, let him have an habitual desire to imitate Christ in everything that he does, conforming himself to His life; upon which life he must meditate so that he may know how to imitate it, and to behave in all things as Christ would behave.

Secondly, in order that he may be able to do this well, every pleasure that presents itself to the senses, if it be not purely for the honour and glory of God, must be renounced and completely rejected for the love of Jesus Christ, Who in this life had no other pleasure, neither desired any, than to do the will of His Father, which He called His meat and food. I take this example. If there present itself to a man the pleasure of listening to things that tend not to the service and honour of God, let him not desire that pleasure, nor desire to listen to them; and if there present itself the pleasure of looking at things that help him not Godward, let him not desire the pleasure or look at these things; and if in conversation or in aught else soever such pleasure present itself, let him act likewise. And similarly with respect to all the senses, in so far as he can fairly avoid the pleasure in question; if he cannot, it suffices that, although these things may be present to his senses, he desires not to have this pleasure. And in this wise he will be able to mortify and void his senses of such pleasure as though they were in darkness. If he takes care to do this, he will soon reap great profit.

For the mortifying and calming of the four natural passions, which are joy, hope, fear and grief, from the concord and pacification whereof come these and other blessings, the counsels here following are of the greatest help, and of great merit, and the source of great virtues.

Strive always to prefer, not that which is easiest, but that which is most difficult;

Not that which is most delectable, but that which is most unpleasing;

Not that which give most pleasure, but rather that which gives least;

Not that which is restful, but that which is wearisome;

Not that which is consolation, but rather that which is disconsolateness;

Not that which is greatest, but that which is least;

Not that which is loftiest and most precious, but that which is lowest and most despised;

Not that which is a desire for anything, but that which is a desire for nothing;

Strive to go about seeking not the best of temporal things, but the worst.

Strive thus to desire to enter into complete detachment and emptiness and poverty, with respect to everything that is in the world, for Christ's sake.

And it is meet that the soul embrace these acts with all its heart and strive to subdue its will thereto. For, if it perform them with its heart, it will very quickly come to find in them great delight and consolation, and to act with order and discretion.

These things that have been said, if they be faithfully put into practice, are quite sufficient for entrance into the night of sense; but, for greater completeness, we shall describe another kind of exercise which teaches us to mortify *the concupiscence of the flesh and the concupiscence of the eyes, and the pride of life,* which, says Saint John [1 Jn. 2, 16], are the things that reign in the world, from which all the other desires proceed.

First, let the soul strive to work in its own despite, and desire all to do so. Secondly, let it strive to speak in its own despite and desire all to do so. Third, let it strive to think humbly of itself, in its own despite, and desire all to do so.

To conclude these counsels and rules, it will be fitting to set down here those lines which are written in the Ascent of the Mount. . . .

In order to arrive at having pleasure in everything,
Desire to have pleasure in nothing.

In order to arrive at possessing everything,
Desire to possess nothing.

In order to arrive at being everything,
Desire to be nothing.

In order to arrive at knowing everything,
Desire to know nothing.

In order to arrive at that wherein thou hast no pleasure,
Thou must go by a way wherein thou hast no pleasure.

In order to arrive at that which thou knowest not,
Thou must go by a way that thou knowest not.

In order to arrive at that which thou possessest not,
Thou must go by a way that thou possessed not.

In order to arrive at that which thou art not,
Thou must go through that which thou art not.

When thy mind dwells upon anything,
Thou art ceasing to cast thyself upon the All.

For, in order to pass from the all to the All,
Thou hast to deny thyself wholly in all.

And, when thou comest to possess it wholly,
Thou must possess it without desiring anything.

For, if thou wilt have anything in having all,
Thou hast not thy treasure purely in God.

In this detachment the spiritual soul finds its quiet and repose; for, since it covets nothing, nothing wearies it when it is lifted up, and nothing oppresses it when it is cast down, because it is in the centre of its humility; but when it covets anything, at that very moment it becomes wearied.

ST. JOHN OF THE CROSS [145]

NOVEMBER 30
ST. ANDREW

When blessed Andrew came to the place where the cross was prepared for him, he exclaimed: "O Good Cross, so long desired and now erected for my longing soul; trusting and rejoicing I come to you; receive me exultingly, disciple of him who hung upon you."

ROMAN BREVIARY [146]

Today is rightly considered St. Andrew's birthday. He did not come to birth from his mother's womb today, but we recognize that through the conception of faith and the child-birth of martyrdom he was brought forth into heavenly glory. His mother's cradle did not receive him today as a softly crying infant, but the heavenly abodes welcomed him in triumph. He did not draw the soft mild nourishment of milk from his mother's breast, but as a devoted soldier he valiantly shed his blood for his King.

He lives, because, as a warrior in the heavenly army, he slew death. Sweating and sighing after his expiring Lord, he follows along and strives to walk with the full vigorous stride of his virtue. Nature had made him similar to his brother [Simon Peter], his vocation had made him a companion, and grace had made him an equal. He did not want this journey to make him dissimilar.

At one word of the Lord, Andrew had, like him, left his father, his country, and his possessions. Through Christ's own gift, he offered himself without wearying as the companion of his brother in labors, reproaches, journeys, insults, and vigils. The only blemish is that he fled at the time of the Lord's Passion. However, his fleeing does not give him an inferior rank. If to deny one's Lord is deemed a fault of some importance, surely it is not more serious to flee than to deny.

We should pass over the other matters in silence, brethren. The forgiveness put on a level those whom their fault had separated. And the fervor with which they afterwards suffered martyrdom proved the devotion of those men who had previously incurred dishonor through their fear. Later on, they eagerly embraced with all their hearts that cross from which they had shrunk, so as to ascend to heaven and gain their reward and crown from the same cross from which they had once derived guilt.

Peter mounted a cross, and Andrew a tree. In this way they who longed to suffer with Christ showed forth in themselves the kind and manner of His suffering; redeemed upon a cross, they were made perfect for their palms. Thus, even if Andrew is second in dignity, he is not inferior in regard to the reward or the suffering.

ST. PETER CHRYSOLOGUS [147]

Andrew was the first of the disciples to know Jesus.

Yet, little as Scripture tells us concerning him, it affords us enough for a lesson, and that an important one. These are the facts before us. St. Andrew was the first convert among the Apostles; he was especially in our Lord's confidence; thrice is he described as introducing others to Him; lastly, he is little known in history, while the place of dignity and the name of highest renown have been allotted to his brother Simon, whom he was the means of bringing to the knowledge of his Saviour.

Our lesson, then, is this; that those men are not necessarily the most useful men in their generation, nor the most favoured by God, who make the most noise in the world, and who seem to be principals in the great changes and events recorded in history; on the contrary, that even when we are able to point to a certain number of men as the real instruments of any great blessings vouchsafed to mankind, our relative estimate of them, one with another, is often very erroneous: so that, on the whole, if we would trace truly the hand of God in human affairs, and pursue His bounty as displayed in the world to its original sources, we must unlearn our admiration of the powerful and distinguished, our reliance on the opinion of society, our respect for the decisions of the learned or the multitude, and turn our eyes to private life, watching in all we read or witness for the true signs of God's presence, the graces of personal holiness manifested in His elect; which, weak as they may seem to mankind, are mighty through God, and have an influence upon the course of His Providence, and bring about great events in the world at large, when the wisdom and strength of the natural man are of no avail. . . .

Why indeed should we shrink from this gracious law of God's present providence in our own case, or in the case of those we love, when our subjection to it does but associate us with the best and noblest of our race, and with beings of nature and condition superior to our own? Andrew is scarcely known except by name; while Peter has ever held the place of honour all over the Church; yet Andrew brought Peter to Christ. And are not the blessed Angels unknown to the world? and is not God Himself, the Author of all good, hid from mankind at large, partially manifested and poorly glorified, in a few scattered servants here and there? and His Spirit, do we know whence It cometh, and whither It goeth? and though He has taught men whatever there has been of wisdom among them from the beginning, yet when He came on earth in visible form, even then it was said of Him, *The world knew Him not.* [Jn. 1, 10] His marvellous providence works beneath a veil, which speaks but an untrue language; and to see Him who is the Truth and the Life, we must stoop underneath it, and so in our turn hide ourselves from the world. They who present themselves at kings' courts, pass on to the inner chambers, where the gaze of the rude multitude cannot pierce; and we, if we would see the King of kings in His glory, must be content to disappear from the things that are seen.

JOHN HENRY NEWMAN [148]

Abbreviations

ACW   *Ancient Christian Writers,* edited by J. Quasten, Walter Burghardt, and T. C. Lawler, Westminster, The Newman Press, 1946–.

ANCL *Ante-Nicene Christian Library,* edited by A. Roberts and and J. Donaldson, Edinburgh, twenty-four volumes, 1867–1884.

ANF   *The Ante-Nicene Fathers,* Edinburgh edition revised by A. C. Coxe, Buffalo, ten volumes, 1884–1886.

FC   *The Fathers of the Church,* founded by L. Schopp, series editor R. J. Deferrari, Washington, D.C., The Catholic University of America Press, 1948–.

LCC   *Library of Christian Classics,* Philadelphia, The Westminster Press.

Reference Table

NUMBER   PAGE

1. Rainer Maria RILKE, in *Rilke, Selected Poems,* Berkeley and Los Angeles, University of California Press, 1962, p. 39.   10

2. John Henry NEWMAN, *Sermons and Discourses, 1839–1857,* edited by C. F. Harrold, II, New York, Longmans, Green, 1949, pp. 17–18.   21

3. Romano GUARDINI, *The Lord,* Chicago, Henry Regnery, 1954, pp. 432–433.   23

218

SANCTORAL

221

224